P9-CBF-514

DISCARD

WEST GA REG LIB SYS
Neva Lomason
Memorial Library

## America's National Parks

# Yellowstone
## National Park

Adventure, Explore, Discover

David Aretha

MyReportLinks.com Books
an imprint of
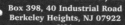
Enslow Publishers, Inc.
Box 398, 40 Industrial Road
Berkeley Heights, NJ 07922
USA

MyReportLinks.com Books, an imprint of Enslow Publishers, Inc. MyReportLinks®
is a registered trademark of Enslow Publishers, Inc.

Copyright © 2009 by Enslow Publishers, Inc.

All rights reserved.

No part of this book may be reproduced by any means
without the written permission of the publisher.

**Library of Congress Cataloging-in-Publication Data**

Aretha, David.
  Yellowstone National Park : adventure, explore, discover / David Aretha.
      p. cm. — (America's national parks)
  Includes bibliographical references and index.
  Audience: Grades 4-6.
  ISBN-13: 978-1-59845-087-3 (hardcover)
  ISBN-10: 1-59845-087-5 (hardcover)
  1. Yellowstone National Park—Juvenile literature.  I. Title.
  F722.A74 2008
  978.7'52—dc22
                              2006103418

Printed in the United States of America

10 9 8 7 6 5 4 3 2 1

**To Our Readers:**
Through the purchase of this book, you and your library gain access to the Report Links that specifically back up this book.
The Publisher will provide access to the Report Links that back up this book and will keep these Report Links up to date on **www.myreportlinks.com** for five years from the book's first publication date.
We have done our best to make sure all Internet addresses in this book were active and appropriate when we went to press. However, the author and the Publisher have no control over, and assume no liability for, the material available on those Internet sites or on other Web sites they may link to.
The usage of the MyReportLinks.com Books Web site is subject to the terms and conditions stated on the Usage Policy Statement on **www.myreportlinks.com**.
A password may be required to access the Report Links that back up this book. The password is found on the bottom of page 4 of this book.
Any comments or suggestions can be sent by e-mail to comments@myreportlinks.com or to the address on the back cover.

✿ Enslow Publishers, Inc., is committed to printing our books on recycled paper. The paper in every book contains 10% to 30% post-consumer waste (PCW). The cover board on the outside of each book contains 100% PCW. Our goal is to do our part to help young people and the environment too!

**Photo Credits:** americanparknetwork.com, p. 110; © Corel Corporation, pp. 7 (bull elk), 33 (Thomas Moran); *Daily Herald,* p. 88; Greater Yellowstone Coalition, p. 82; © iStockphoto.com (Steve Geer), pp. 3 & 8–9 (Old Faithful), 6 (Grand Canyon of the Yellowstone) & 94 (Amar Veuri), 6 (wolf) & 80 (Len Tillim), 54–55 (Craig Cozart), 77 (Kriss Russell); © James S. Macdonald Jr., p. 39; Library of Congress, pp. 26, 34; mtmen.org, p. 25; MyReportLinks.com Books, p. 4; *National Geographic,* p. 106; National Park Service/Enslow Publishers, Inc., p. 5; National Park Service, pp. 6 (trout), 7 (Yellowstone River photo/Ed Austin & Herb Jones), 15, 16–17 (Jim Peaco), 18, 31, 32 (William H. Jackson), 36–37, 38, 42, 48, 50, 51, 56–57 (Austin & Jones), 62, 65 (Harlan Kredit), 74–75, 87 & 92 (Jim Peaco), 100 (JW Stockert); National Parks Conservation Association, p. 85; National Wildlife Federation, p. 72; PBS, pp. 22, 24; Photos.com, pp. 12–13; Science Daily, p. 68; © Shutterstock.com, pp. 1 (GSK), 6–7 (top banner photo of Lower Falls/GSK), 7 (bison/Jerry Sharp), 16–17 (laptop), 28–29, 53 (Sascha Burkard), 54–55 (camcorder), 69 (Tony Campbell), 80–81 (camera), 94–95 (Palm Pilot), 98 (Lane V. Erickson); Sierra Club, p. 59; shoshoneindian.com, p. 21; terragalleria.com, p. 104; USGS, pp. 19, 47, 78; US-Parks.com, p. 10, 70; Yellowstone Association, p. 90; yellowstonenationalpark .com, p. 67; Yellowstone National Park Research Coordination Network/Montana State University, p. 61; Yellowstonepark.com, p. 96; The Yellowstone Park Foundation, p. 114.

**Cover Photo:** © Shutterstock.com/ GSK

**Cover Description:** The Grand Canyon of Yellowstone

# CONTENTS

About MyReportLinks.com Books . . . . . . . .  4

Map of Yellowstone National Park . . . . . . .  5

Yellowstone National Park Facts . . . . . . . .  6

**1** WONDERLAND . . . . . . . . . . . . . . . . . . .  8

**2** EVOLUTION AND EXPLORATION . . . . . . . .  16

**3** A HISTORY OF THE PARK . . . . . . . . . . .  36

**4** WILDERNESS AND WILDLIFE . . . . . . . . .  54

**5** HOT-BUTTON ISSUES . . . . . . . . . . . . . .  80

**6** ENDLESS ADVENTURES . . . . . . . . . . . . .  94

Report Links . . . . . . . . . . . . . . . . . . . . 118

Glossary . . . . . . . . . . . . . . . . . . . . . . 120

Chapter Notes . . . . . . . . . . . . . . . . . . . 122

Further Reading . . . . . . . . . . . . . . . . . . 125

Index . . . . . . . . . . . . . . . . . . . . . . . . 126

# MyReportLinks.com Books
## Great Books, Great Links, Great for Research!

**T**he Internet sites featured in this book can save you hours of research time. These Internet sites—we call them **"Report Links"**—are constantly changing, but we keep them up to date on our Web site.

When you see this "Approved Web Site" logo, you will know that we are directing you to a great Internet site that will help you with your research.

Give it a try! Type http://www.myreportlinks.com into your browser, click on the series title and enter the password, then click on the book title, and scroll down to the Report Links listed for this book.

The Report Links will bring you to great source documents, photographs, and illustrations. MyReportLinks.com Books save you time, feature Report Links that are kept up to date, and make report writing easier than ever! A complete listing of the Report Links can be found on pages 118–119 at the back of the book.

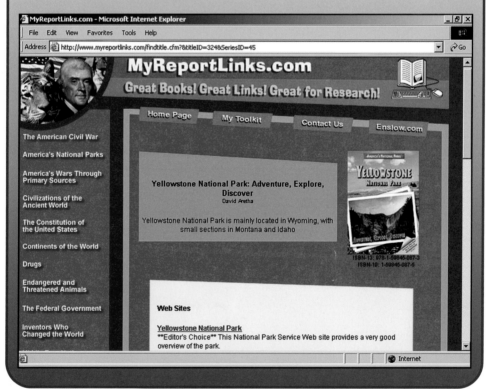

Please see "To Our Readers" on the copyright page for important information about this book, the MyReportLinks.com Web site, and the Report Links that back up this book.

Please enter **YNP1628** if asked for a password.

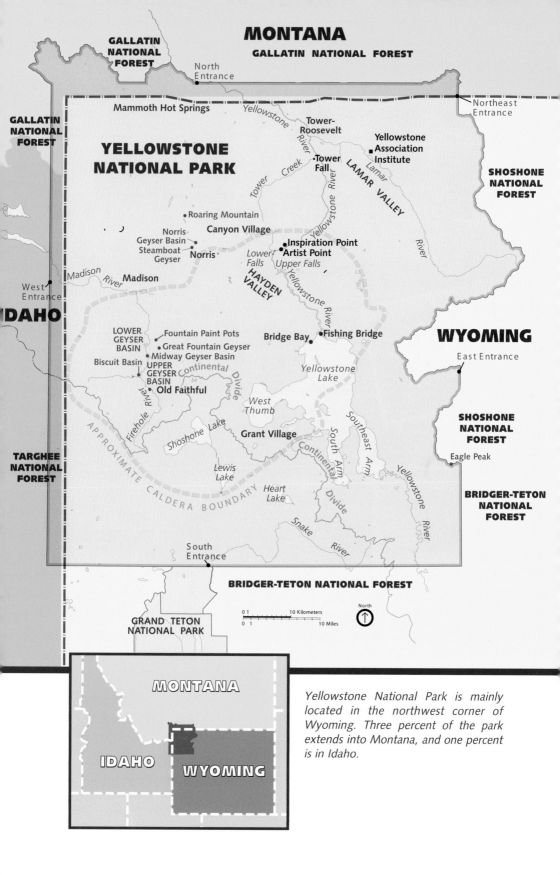

Yellowstone National Park is mainly located in the northwest corner of Wyoming. Three percent of the park extends into Montana, and one percent is in Idaho.

- Yellowstone became the United States' (and the world's) first national park in 1872.

- The park was designated a Biosphere Reserve Site in 1976, and a World Heritage Site in 1978.

- Yellowstone National Park encompasses 3,472 square miles (8,987 square kilometers) and 2,221,766 acres (899,117 hectares).

- It extends 63 miles (102 kilometers) north to south, and 54 miles (87 kilometers) east to west.

- The park is larger than the state of Delaware.

- Ninety-six percent of the park is in Wyoming, 3 percent is in Montana, and one percent is in Idaho.

- Eagle Peak is its highest point at 11,358 feet (3,462 meters).

- Reese Creek is its lowest point at 5,282 feet (1,610 meters).

- Eighty percent of the park is forested, 15 percent is grassland, and 5 percent is covered by water.

- Record high temperature is 98°F (37°C) in 1936.

- Record low temperature is −66°F (−54°C) in 1933.

- The park experiences approximately two thousand small earthquakes per year.

- Yellowstone is home to roughly ten thousand hydrothermal features, including more than three hundred geysers.

# PARK FACTS

- Much of the park rests on one of the world's largest calderas, which measures 45 × 30 miles (72 × 48 kilometers).

- It includes approximately 290 waterfalls, the tallest of which is Lower Falls of the Yellowstone River at 308 feet (94 meters).

- Yellowstone Lake measures 136 square miles (352 square kilometers).

- The park includes five entrances, 466 miles (750 kilometers) of roads, and 950 miles (1,529 kilometers) of backcountry trails.

- Park facilities include nine visitor centers and museums, nine hotels/lodges, seven National Park Service-operated campgrounds and five concession-operated campgrounds, forty-nine picnic areas, and one marina.

- Approximately 800 National Park Service employees work at Yellowstone, while another 3,700 work for concessions.

- Yellowstone attracts close to 3 million visitors each year. The record is 3,144,405 in 1992.

- Wintertime attendance is usually around 140,000.

- Seven-day admission is $25 per vehicle or $12 per hiker or cyclist.

- Mailing address: National Park Service, P.O. Box 168, Yellowstone National Park, WY 82190-0168.

# Chapter 1

An eruption of Old Faithful, the most famous geyser in Yellowstone.

# Wonderland

**S**teve Watson of Los Angeles made his first journey to the legendary Yellowstone National Park. All his life, he had heard and read of its wonders. It could not, he thought, live up to all the hype.

"I expected to see something [along the lines of] the old Disney movies about Yellowstone and other parks," he wrote. "[I expected] something kind of hokey, interesting but not fascinating, in a sort of cheesy, touristy setting. It was anything but that!"[1]

As Watson passed the gates, he journeyed through a land of mountains and valleys, forests and wildflowers. This was a paradise of lakes and rivers, a grand canyon and thundering waterfalls. And through it all, steaming water swirled in colorful hot pools, and geysers blasted into the air. At one point, Watson visited Old Faithful, the most famous geyser in the world.

"The setting was spectacular," he wrote, "and when Old Faithful erupted, it was mesmerizing! Thunderous, powerful, beautiful. It was, to use an old phrase, awe-inspiring!"[2]

"I've been back to Old Faithful many times since," Watson continued, "and each time I'm amazed at how fantastic it is. I've spent time on the boardwalks around Old Faithful watching other geysers and thermal features as well, and they are all truly spectacular."[3]

Many geologic and hydrothermal wonders of the park, including Mammoth Hot Springs, Norris Geyser Basin, and mudpots are discussed at **U.S. National Parks & Monuments Travel Guide: Yellowstone National Park.** Features of the site also include a volcano question and answer session, an article on the Greater Yellowstone Ecosystem, and visitor information.

Old Faithful is one of the many reasons why Congress made Yellowstone America's—and actually, the world's—first national park back in 1872. The park is enormous, covering 3,472 square miles (2.2 million acres). Ninety-six percent of Yellowstone National Park lies in the northwest corner of Wyoming. Parts of the park also lie in Montana (3 percent) and Idaho (1 percent).

Yellowstone National Park is the heart of the Greater Yellowstone Ecosystem, one of the largest intact temperate ecosystems in the world. Surrounding the park are other large, federally protected areas. They include the Grand Teton National Park to the south and several national forests: Bridger-Teton, Shoshone, Targhee, Beaverhead, Custer, and Gallatin. The Jedediah Smith Wilderness Area lies to the west, while the National Elk Refuge was established to the immediate south. Thus, the park is not unnaturally sectioned off. Much of Yellowstone's wildlife is free to roam to these nearby protected areas.

## America's Favorite Getaway

Over the years, America's entertainment options have skyrocketed. Hundreds of resorts, theme parks, and luxury hotels have opened nationwide. Yet despite such competition, Yellowstone's popularity steadily increased and has remained strong. Park attendance rose from about 1 million in 1948 to 2.1 million in 1965 to 3.1 million in 1992. Current annual attendance continues to hover close to 3 million.

With vacation spots like Las Vegas and Disney World to choose from, why do so many Americans continue to flock to Yellowstone? In short, it is America's getaway. Americans live in a nation of

Bison graze peacefully in one of Yellowstone's meadows. Trees damaged by a fire can be seen on the hillside at right.

factories and congested roadways, pollution and construction. Their schools, offices, and even their homes can be sources of stress. If people want to get away—truly get away—they go to Yellowstone rather than to a more commercialized top vacation spot. There they can camp under the stars and awake to the sights, sounds, and scents of

pure nature. Yellowstone does have roads, hotels, and other facilities, but 97 percent of the park is wilderness.

Yellowstone's management team works diligently to preserve the natural state of the park. Yet Yellowstone National Park was originally created for the enjoyment of the public. Tourists come for the assorted outdoor activities. At Yellowstone, they can fish for trout or boat on Yellowstone Lake. They can ride horses in the park and ski during the winter. Hikers can choose from 950 miles of back-country trails.

Even people who are not physically active can enjoy a glorious vacation at Yellowstone. It is a sightseer's dream come true. As John Muir wrote in *Our National Parks:* "The air is electric and full of ozone, healing, reviving, exhilarating, kept pure by frost and fire, while the scenery is wild enough to awaken the dead."[4]

At Yellowstone, such captivating, formidable animals as the elk, bison, coyote, and gray wolf run wild. Endangered bald eagles with seven-foot wingspans soar proudly above. The views are unimaginably breathtaking, from the snow-capped mountain peaks to the plunging depths of the canyons. All the while, Yellowstone's hydrothermal features—from hissing steam vents to eruptive geysers—seem out of this world.

**Windows Into Wonderland: Yellowstone National Park** presents a collection of seventeen multimedia field trips. Subjects include wildlife of the park such as wolves, bears, goats, and trumpeter swans. A history of the park, a quest for geysers, and the ecology of fire are also featured.

**EDITOR'S CHOICE**

"It is a vast area of earthly riches almost beyond imagining," wrote Tim Cahill in *Lost in My Own Backyard,* "a natural playground complete with geysers and thermal features so strange that early white visitors referred to the area as 'Wonderland.'"[5]

How is it that such an array of natural wonders is concentrated in one location? Let's go back millions of years to see how it all began.

# Chapter

## 2

A view of the Grand Prismatic Spring located in Midway Geyser Basin. At 370 feet (113 meters) in diameter, it is the third largest hot spring in the world.

# Evolution and Exploration

**W**hen the historic Washburn expedition entered the Yellowstone area in 1870, they named a certain hot-spring location Hell-Broth Springs. A member of the expedition, Cornelius Hedges, wrote: "[It's] doubtless [that] the sources of this heat, if not of the water, are the great internal fires in the innermost bowels of the earth."[1] Scientists would later confirm Hedges's assumption. Yellowstone was created by three supervolcanos over the last 2 million years. These eruptions were the largest on the earth over that period of time.

To fully understand the Yellowstone story, we must travel back a hundred million years. Around that time, two of the dozen or so enormous sections of the earth's crust collided: the Pacific plate

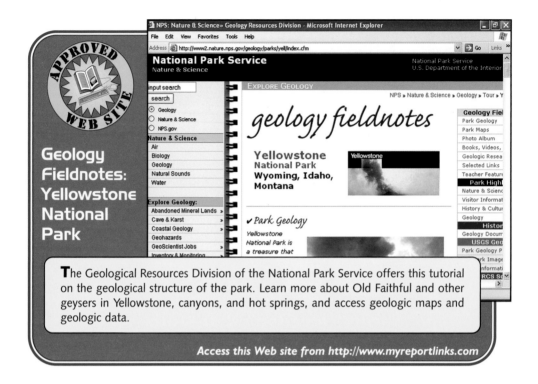

**Geology Fieldnotes: Yellowstone National Park**

The Geological Resources Division of the National Park Service offers this tutorial on the geological structure of the park. Learn more about Old Faithful and other geysers in Yellowstone, canyons, and hot springs, and access geologic maps and geologic data.

*Access this Web site from http://www.myreportlinks.com*

rammed into the North American plate. In fact, the Pacific plate moved under the North American plate, causing tremendous volcanic activity and forming the Rocky Mountains, of which Yellowstone is a part.

About 2.2 million years ago, a major geologic event occurred in the Yellowstone area. A massive amount of magma, or melted rock, about sixty miles wide blasted through the earth's crust and erupted into the atmosphere. The ash and debris that spewed out fused together, forming a light-colored volcanic rock called rhyolite. More than sixteen hundred square miles were buried by rhyolite a thousand feet thick.

## ⊖THE BIG ONE

About 1.3 million years ago, a second massive eruption occurred in what is now Idaho, along Yellowstone's western boundary. The third and most significant of the three supervolcanos last erupted about 640,000 years ago. It ejected eight thousand times as much ash as Mount St. Helens did in 1980. As the rock settled, it formed a huge depression called a caldera, which was a mile deep. Most of Yellowstone lies within it. At twenty-eight by forty-seven miles wide, it is the world's largest crater valley.

For many thousands of years, more volcanic activity continued to occur in the area, which is

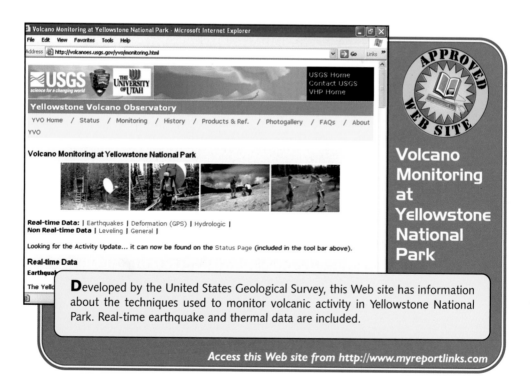

**Volcano Monitoring at Yellowstone National Park**

Developed by the United States Geological Survey, this Web site has information about the techniques used to monitor volcanic activity in Yellowstone National Park. Real-time earthquake and thermal data are included.

*Access this Web site from http://www.myreportlinks.com*

still considered a "hot spot." While the earth's crust is more than twenty miles thick in most places, it is only several miles thick at Yellowstone. Below it lies boiling hot magma. This heat seeps through cracks in the crust, heating ground water that results in the park's fumaroles, geysers, hot springs, and mud pots. The ice ages in this area (three of them from about 300,000 to 12,500 years ago) also shaped the land of Yellowstone, forming canyons and valleys.

When the last major ice age ended, the Yellowstone area included more than thirty mountains that were at least ten thousand feet high. It also featured many volcanic plateaus that are currently more than a mile high. The area remains extremely volatile, as it averages more than fifteen earthquakes per year. Those do not include the many microquakes that regularly rock the park. Despite its serene beauty, Yellowstone is among the most unpredictable places on Earth.

## ⊜ THE FIRST HUMAN INHABITANTS

Humans first witnessed the splendor of Yellowstone approximately eleven thousand years ago. The area's mountainous, forested terrain and its cold winters made it a difficult place to live. However, that did not stop a band of Western Shoshone Indians known as the Sheep Eaters, or the Tukuaduka. They settled in the area as early

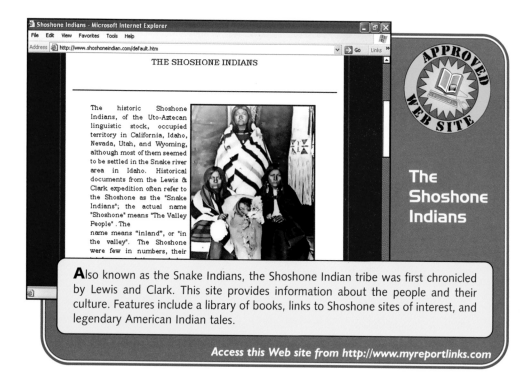

THE SHOSHONE INDIANS

The historic Shoshone Indians, of the Uto-Aztecan linguistic stock, occupied territory in California, Idaho, Nevada, Utah, and Wyoming, although most of them seemed to be settled in the Snake river area in Idaho. Historical documents from the Lewis & Clark expedition often refer to the Shoshone as the "Snake Indians"; the actual name "Shoshone" means "The Valley People". The name means "inland", or "in the valley". The Shoshone were few in numbers, their

**The Shoshone Indians**

**A**lso known as the Snake Indians, the Shoshone Indian tribe was first chronicled by Lewis and Clark. This site provides information about the people and their culture. Features include a library of books, links to Shoshone sites of interest, and legendary American Indian tales.

*Access this Web site from http://www.myreportlinks.com*

as the time of Christ, more than two thousand years ago. This band hunted Rocky Mountain bighorn sheep, made bows from the sheep's horns, and lived in shelters called wikiups. As late as 1835, fur trapper Osborne Russell encountered the Sheep Eaters. He noted that they were "neatly clothed in dressed deer and sheepskins of the best quality and seemed to be perfectly happy."[2] In the early 1800s, the Sheep Eaters traded with fur trappers and told them where they could find beavers.

In the 1700s and 1800s, more and more American Indians moved west toward the area. Some called the region Yellow Stone due to the yellow

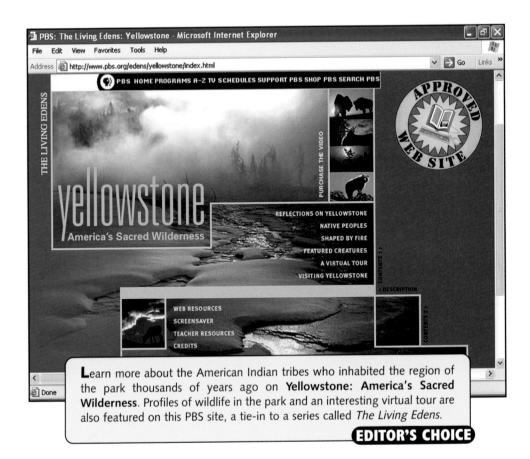

PBS: The Living Edens: Yellowstone - Microsoft Internet Explorer

File    Edit    View    Favorites    Tools    Help

Address http://www.pbs.org/edens/yellowstone/index.html    Go    Links

PBS HOME PROGRAMS A–Z TV SCHEDULES SUPPORT PBS SHOP PBS SEARCH PBS

THE LIVING EDENS

**yellowstone**
America's Sacred Wilderness

PURCHASE THE VIDEO

REFLECTIONS ON YELLOWSTONE
NATIVE PEOPLES
SHAPED BY FIRE
FEATURED CREATURES
A VIRTUAL TOUR
VISITING YELLOWSTONE

‹ DESCRIPTION

WEB RESOURCES
SCREENSAVER
TEACHER RESOURCES
CREDITS

APPROVED WEB SITE

Done

**L**earn more about the American Indian tribes who inhabited the region of the park thousands of years ago on **Yellowstone: America's Sacred Wilderness**. Profiles of wildlife in the park and an interesting virtual tour are also featured on this PBS site, a tie-in to a series called *The Living Edens*.

**EDITOR'S CHOICE**

sandstone bluffs near present-day Billings, Montana. Others referred to the region as Smoke from the Ground. Few American Indians made their home in the heart of Yellowstone. Instead, they made occasional forays into the area to hunt and forage for food. Members of the Crow, a horse-riding tribe, lived around Yellowstone's eastern boundary. The Blackfeet, an aggressive and feared tribe, lived to the north in Montana and Alberta, Canada.

### ⮕ WHITE MEN EXPLORE THE REGION

Historians believe that no white person (meaning someone of European descent) ever saw Yellowstone until after 1800. However, one Canadian voyager heard about the amazing region by talking to American Indians. In 1796, Jean Baptiste Trudeau described what he had learned about the Yellowstone River: "Its banks are well supplied with wood. There are found firs, pines, North American firs, birches, cedars, and every other tree. The buffalo and other wild animals rove in herds along its banks. Many little rivers that flow into it abound in beaver beyond all belief."[3]

In 1803, Yellowstone officially became American territory. With that year's Louisiana Purchase, the United States acquired the area—actually the central third of the current United States—from France. In August 1803, Meriwether Lewis and William Clark began their famous expedition to explore western territory. They journeyed past the outer fringes of the region but did not enter Yellowstone.

However, John Colter, a member of the Lewis and Clark expedition, explored the Yellowstone area from 1807 to 1810. Colter told tales of the hot steaming springs and geysers in the area, which eventually became known as Colter's Hell. Other mountain men would soon follow in his footsteps.

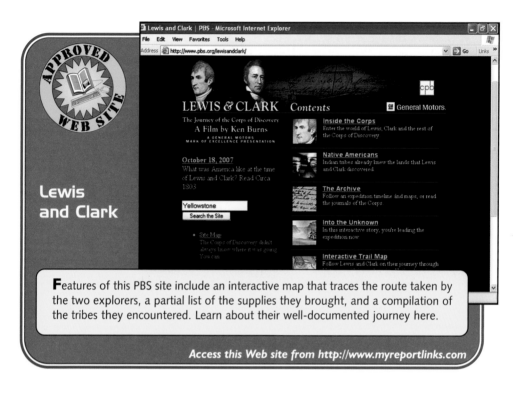

Features of this PBS site include an interactive map that traces the route taken by the two explorers, a partial list of the supplies they brought, and a compilation of the tribes they encountered. Learn about their well-documented journey here.

*Access this Web site from http://www.myreportlinks.com*

## ➔ "WILD, ROMANTIC SPLENDOR"

Trappers and other adventurers were the next to explore, map, and describe Yellowstone. Alexander Ross wrote in 1819 that "[b]oiling fountains having different degrees of temperature were very numerous; one or two were so very hot as to boil meat."[4]

Fellow trappers considered such accounts ridiculous—until they experienced Yellowstone themselves. Legendary mountain man Joe Meek described the hot springs district in 1829 as "larger craters, some of them from four to six miles across. Out of these craters, issued blue flames and molten brimstone."[5]

For decades, only the occasional explorer would visit Yellowstone. In the 1830s, a literate easterner named Osborne Russell provided the first detailed accounts of the region. He described not just the geyser basins but the wildlife and gorgeous vistas. As he wrote in 1835: "We stopped at this place and for my own part I almost wished I could spend the remainder of my days in a place like this, where happiness and contentment seemed to reign in wild, romantic splendor, surrounded by majestic battlements which seemed to support the heavens and shut out all hostile intruders."[6]

Very gradually, Americans learned about this fantastic oasis. Jim Bridger, the most famous of all

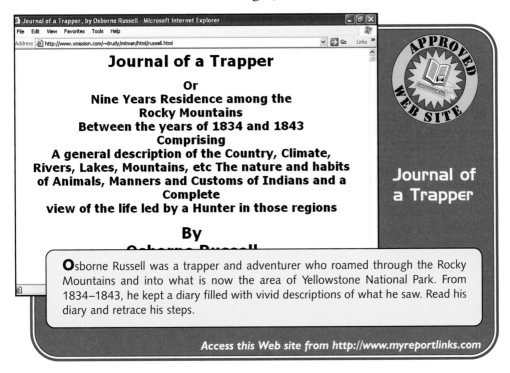

Journal of a Trapper, by Osborne Russell - Microsoft Internet Explorer

File   Edit   View   Favorites   Tools   Help

Address   http://www.xmission.com/~drudy/mtman/html/russell.html   Go   Links »

## Journal of a Trapper

### Or
### Nine Years Residence among the
### Rocky Mountains
### Between the years of 1834 and 1843
### Comprising
### A general description of the Country, Climate,
### Rivers, Lakes, Mountains, etc The nature and habits
### of Animals, Manners and Customs of Indians and a
### Complete
### view of the life led by a Hunter in those regions

### By

Journal of a Trapper

**O**sborne Russell was a trapper and adventurer who roamed through the Rocky Mountains and into what is now the area of Yellowstone National Park. From 1834–1843, he kept a diary filled with vivid descriptions of what he saw. Read his diary and retrace his steps.

*Access this Web site from http://www.myreportlinks.com*

mountain men, spread the word after exploring Yellowstone in the 1840s. "Come with me to Yellowstone next summer," Bridger proclaimed, "and I'll show you peetrified [sic] trees a-growing, with peetrified birds on 'em a-singing peetrified songs."[7]

Captain J. W. Gunnison reported more of Bridger's descriptions of the region: "Geysers spout up seventy feet high with a terrific, hissing noise, at regular intervals. . . . On the other side is an acid spring, which gushes out in a river torrent; and below is a cave, which supplies 'vermillion' for the savages in abundance."[8]

In 1859, the U.S. government sponsored an expedition to Yellowstone. Captain W. F. Raynolds,

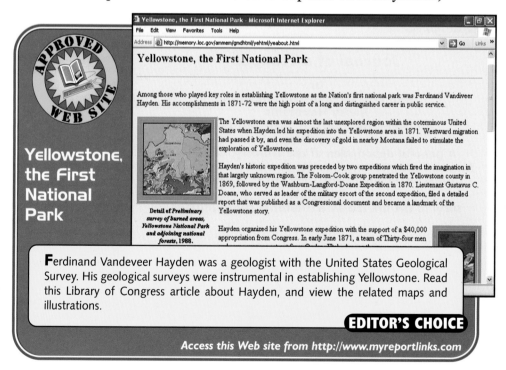

Yellowstone, the First National Park

Ferdinand Vandeveer Hayden was a geologist with the United States Geological Survey. His geological surveys were instrumental in establishing Yellowstone. Read this Library of Congress article about Hayden, and view the related maps and illustrations.

**EDITOR'S CHOICE**

Access this Web site from http://www.myreportlinks.com

a U.S. army surveyor, led the way, with Bridger serving as his guide and Ferdinand V. Hayden serving as the group's geologist, naturalist, and surgeon. Unfortunately, heavy snow—which had fallen as late as June—prevented them from entering the region. As Raynolds lamented, "[W]e were compelled to content ourselves with listening to marvelous tales of burning plains, immense lakes, and boiling springs. . . ."[9]

## ➲ THE FIRST EXPEDITIONS

In the wake of the California gold rush that began in 1848, prospectors moved out across the West in search of more of the precious treasure. In the early 1860s, miners struck it rich in the mountains of Montana. Throughout the decade, many prospectors passed through the Yellowstone region. Some stayed and searched for gold, although with disappointing results. Most importantly, these men wrote extensively about the region, raving about what they called "Wonderland." All this buzz about Yellowstone inspired three men—David Folsom, Charles W. Cook, and William Peterson—to launch an exploration of the area.

Loaded with guns for hunting and protection, the trio examined the region thoroughly beginning September 6, 1869. They explored Yellowstone River, the Falls of Yellowstone, the Lower Geyser

The colorful Emerald Pool discovered by Henry Washburn and his expedition in 1870.

Basin, and many other highlights during a thirty-six day expedition. In compelling detail, Folsom wrote about the wonders he had witnessed in *Western Monthly.*

Montana Surveyor General and former Congressman Henry D. Washburn was sufficiently intrigued. On August 22, 1870, with Nathaniel P. Langford and a U.S. Army escort led by Lieutenant Gustavus C. Doane, Washburn conducted a historic expedition—one that would directly lead to the dedication of the world's first national park.

Throughout their journey, the men bestowed grand names upon the park's features. They christened one geyser Giantess and another Splendid, and they named colorful hot pools Emerald and Sapphire. Washburn's senses were overwhelmed by Giantess. "Standing near the fountain when in motion, and the sun shining, the scene is grandly magnificent," the general explained. "Each of the broken atoms of water shining . . . while myriads of rainbows are dancing attendance. No wonder, then, that our usually staid and sober companions threw up their hats and shouted with ecstasy at the sight."[10]

## ➲THE WORD SPREADS EAST

Others on the trek were similarly impressed. Upon experiencing Old Faithful, Lieutenant Gustavus C. Doane exclaimed, "The earth affords not its equal. It is the most lovely inanimate object in existence."[11] On December 15, 1870, Doane finished his report on the journey and sent it to General Tecumseh Sherman in Washington, D.C. Soon, reports about Yellowstone were published in the East.

Nathaniel P. Langford wrote articles about Yellowstone for national magazines. He told the amazing story of Washburn expedition member Truman Everts, a former tax agent, who got lost as the team explored the south side of Yellowstone Lake. Everts wandered aimlessly for days, living on grass and roots. During chilly nights, the hot springs kept him warm. He supposedly weighed only fifty pounds before he was finally rescued.

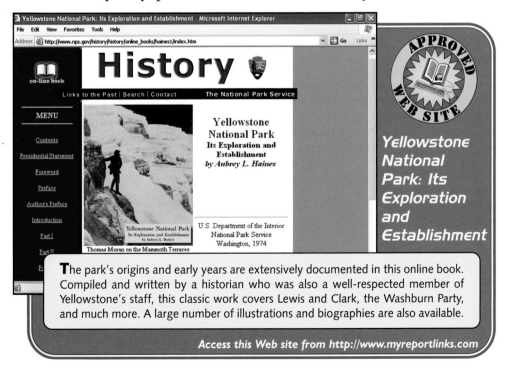

*Yellowstone National Park: Its Exploration and Establishment*

The park's origins and early years are extensively documented in this online book. Compiled and written by a historian who was also a well-respected member of Yellowstone's staff, this classic work covers Lewis and Clark, the Washburn Party, and much more. A large number of illustrations and biographies are also available.

*Access this Web site from http://www.myreportlinks.com*

Throughout the East, readers were entranced by other articles describing fossil forests, a mountain composed of volcanic glass, and a colorful gorge with two stunning waterfalls.

The federal government, too, was intrigued. In 1871, the U.S. Geological Survey sponsored two expeditions to the newfound wonderland. Ferdinand Hayden headed one, and Captains Barlow and Heap of the Engineer Corps of the Army led the other. Together, they compiled a large collection of data about the region. Perhaps more importantly, photographer William Henry Jackson

William H. Jackson's 1871 painting of the Hayden expedition from the Yellowstone National Park collection. Geologist Ferdinand Hayden's 1870 expedition was one of many to the Yellowstone area.

▲ *Artist Thomas Moran painted the splendor of the Grand Canyon of Yellowstone in this landscape from 1872. Moran's paintings were shown to Congress to help convince members to enact legislation naming Yellowstone the first national park.*

and artist Thomas Moran—legendary figures— recorded the splendors of Yellowstone in photographs and paintings.

## ⊜THE FIRST NATIONAL PARK

Throughout the early 1870s, a move was on to preserve the Yellowstone region. However, neither the Montana nor Wyoming territories could lay claim to Yellowstone because it overlapped both of

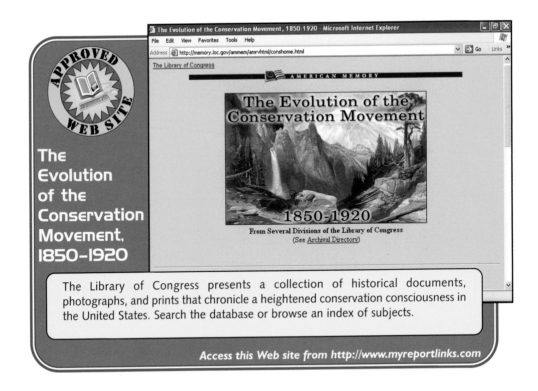

APPROVED WEB SITE

The
Evolution
of the
Conservation
Movement,
1850-1920

The Library of Congress presents a collection of historical documents, photographs, and prints that chronicle a heightened conservation consciousness in the United States. Search the database or browse an index of subjects.

**Access this Web site from http://www.myreportlinks.com**

them. Only the federal government could take action. After the completion of the 1871 expeditions in October, deal-makers in Washington worked to create legislation to establish Yellowstone National Park.

William Clagett, who had recently been elected a delegate to Congress from Montana, took the lead. On December 18, 1871, he submitted the National Park Bill to the U.S. House of Representatives. To sway the members of Congress, Hayden delivered impressive photographs of Yellowstone to all the senators and representatives. They couldn't resist. The bill was adopted by the House on January 30, 1872, and was passed by the Senate on February 27. On March 1, 1872, President Ulysses S. Grant signed the bill into law.

Prior to that historic day, the government previously had acted to preserve land. However, the purpose of the preservation had been to conserve materials of industry, such as coal and iron. But now the government acted to preserve land because of its pure beauty. According to the act, Yellowstone National Park was "dedicated and set apart as a public park or pleasuring-ground for the benefit and enjoyment of the people."[12]

Across the nation, Americans celebrated the news. But important questions remained. Yellowstone National Park was spread out over more than three thousand square miles. Who was going to maintain it—and how?

# Chapter

# 3

Visitors to the National Hotel at Mammoth Hot Springs are shown in a stagecoach in this undated photograph from the National Park Service archives.

# A History of the Park

**N**athaniel P. Langford, a leading advocate for the creation of Yellowstone National Park, was named its first superintendent in 1872. Langford boasted that his initials, N.P., stood for "National Park." However, in his five years as superintendent, Langford visited the park only two or three times and wrote only one report.

In reality, Langford could do little. He received neither a salary nor a budget for running the park. No one maintained or guarded Yellowstone, and the result was pure chaos.

During Langford's reign, hunters enjoyed a field day. As General William E. Strong wrote, "An elk skin is worth from six to eight dollars, and it is said that when the snow is deep, and a herd gets confused, one hunter will frequently kill from twenty-five to fifty of these noble animals in a single day."[1] In the spring of 1875, the Bottler brothers (three Dutch men with a ranch in Paradise Valley where other hunters often stayed) were responsible for killing more than two thousand elk.

Hunters also killed mountain sheep, deer, bison, and other animals. In addition, visitors vandalized the park. Tourists crammed logs, rocks,

▲ Nathaniel Langford, who took part in the famous Washburn expedition, wrote about Yellowstone and later became the park's first superintendent in 1872.

and garments into geysers. They poured in soap and laughed at the eruptions. Others took home petrified trees as souvenirs.

## ⊙ YELLOWSTONE'S SUPPORTERS

In 1877, Philetus Norris took over as Yellowstone's superintendent. He could do little to control visitors' behavior, but he was able to improve the park's infrastructure. In 1878, Congress approved a salary for the park's superintendent as well as a ten-thousand-dollar budget to protect, preserve, and improve the park. Norris used the money to build roads and trails for visitors.

In 1880, Norris hired Harry Yount as game warden. However, Yount quit because he couldn't

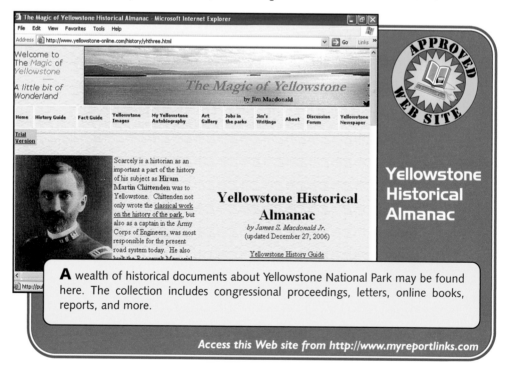

**A** wealth of historical documents about Yellowstone National Park may be found here. The collection includes congressional proceedings, letters, online books, reports, and more.

*Access this Web site from http://www.myreportlinks.com*

regulate all the uncontrolled hunting and fishing. Even Secretary of the Interior Hoke Smith indulged in excess. In 1883, Smith caught two hundred fish in one day. The situation was completely out of hand. Five thousand tourists per year did as they pleased. Some carved their names in hot springs basins. Developers established bath and laundry facilities at the hot springs. Others ran amusement rides and sold souvenirs.

Railroad companies wanted to exploit the park even further. They spent millions of dollars constructing tracks that, by 1892, would lead to within three miles of Yellowstone's Gardiner entrance. Their dream was to continue the railroad through the park, right up to such attractions as Old Faithful.

## ⊜ PUTTING THE BRAKES ON THE RAILROADS

General Philip Sheridan, a Civil War hero, emerged as a champion for the park. He informed the public about Yellowstone's lack of supervision and the abuse of its wildlife. He also convinced the secretary of the interior to forbid railroad construction within the park. For years, members of Congress debated this issue, but the preservationists always won. As Senator George Vest said, "[A]llowing any railroad to enter Yellowstone would end in the destruction of the Park."[2] Eventually, the best that railroad magnates would do was to extend track up to a Yellowstone entrance.

By 1886, scandals plagued Yellowstone National Park. Besides rampant destruction and poaching, criminals such as stagecoach robbers infested the park. Members of Congress were so disgusted that they withheld park funding for the year. As a reaction to that decision, park employees started forest fires and damaged public facilities. Finally, the army came to the rescue.

## ➡ THE ARMY TAKES CONTROL

That August, Captain Moses Harris and his troops took control of Yellowstone. The army kicked out squatters and ordered hunters to cease their poaching. Illegal activity decreased even further thanks to a new law enacted in 1894. This law, called the Lacey Act, basically made it a crime to kill or harm Yellowstone's animals.

Not only did the army police the park effectively, but it improved the area as well. In 1885, the Army Corps of Engineers completed Yellowstone's Golden Gate Bridge. The army also created plans to help specific animals thrive in the park.

When Yellowstone's bison population dwindled to about twenty-five, the remaining bison were herded into a large fenced area in Lamar Valley. Eventually, the number of bison multiplied. (Today, several thousand roam the park.) The park's overseers also hired companies to kill the park's animal predators, including mountain lions and coyotes. The army ruled Yellowstone for thirty years and did not leave until the end of World War I.

## GRAND TOUR OF WONDERLAND

During the last two decades of the nineteenth century, thousands of well-to-do tourists visited Yellowstone. They came from the big cities of the West, such as San Francisco and Denver, and even from the East Coast. The railroads offered special packages for the "Grand Tour of Wonderland." The Northern Pacific Railroad took vacationers via rail to Cinnabar, Montana, three miles from Yellowstone. From there, visitors traveled via

▲ The Old Faithful Inn was constructed in the winter of 1903–04. This historic photo was taken in 1912.

stagecoach to the park. Over periods of five or six days, tourists slept in hotels and toured the sites in the coaches.

In the early years, lodging accommodations were primitive. Guests at the "hotels" were forced to sleep on the floor. The Firehole Hotel offered beds, but its walls were made of canvas. Not until 1883, with the opening of the fabulous National Hotel at Mammoth Hot Springs, did wealthy tourists feel at home. More lavish buildings followed. The Fountain Hotel opened in the Upper Geyser Basin in 1891. It featured luxuries such as steam heat, electric lights, and hot water for baths. In 1904, the Old Faithful Inn opened for business.

In the evenings, tourists dined in style. A 1908 menu of the Lake Hotel offered a multi-course dinner. Here is a sampling of what was served:

*Potage a'la Maryland*
*Baked lake trout a'la bordelaise*
*Lamb kidneys saute a'la Rachel*
*Roast prime ribs of beef au jus*
*Carrotes a'la Vichy*
*Turkish figs*
*Chocolate cream fritters*
*Coffee, cocoa, tea, or milk* [3]

## FRIENDLY RANGERS

By 1916, the number of national parks in the United States had grown to thirty. To manage them all, Congress established the National Park Service (NPS) that year. When the army left Yellowstone in 1918, NPS personnel took control of the park.

The new park rangers probably seemed more welcoming than the army troops. Rangers greeted visitors at the park's entrance gates. They patrolled the vast acreage on foot, horseback, and later by motorcycle. They maintained public facilities and managed the park's wildlife. And if a tourist suffered an injury, a ranger was quick to the scene with first-aid supplies.

## AGE OF THE AUTOMOBILE

In 1915, automobiles were allowed to enter through the gates of Yellowstone National Park. Very quickly, convertible motor buses replaced the dusty stagecoaches. *Motor West* magazine stated that Yellowstone's animals would have to get accustomed to the "invasion of these strange monsters from the outer world."[4] Indeed, it wasn't long before the automobile became the preferred mode of travel through the grand wonderland.

In the early years of auto travel, Yellowstone drivers faced strict limitations. They had to pull over whenever a stagecoach approached. Speed limits ranged from a high of fifteen miles per hour to just six miles per hour in treacherous areas. However, the condition of the roads was so poor that the speed limit didn't matter.

Nevertheless, auto tourists were delighted with the sights of Yellowstone. While cruising in the most modern of vehicles, they could indulge in the park's natural beauty. As a writer in *American Motorist* magazine stated in 1915: "The grade to Mount Washburn is not too steep for the average motor, and there is an exclamation point at every turn. Here the road hugs the cliff above a sheer drop of a thousand feet. There it suddenly swerves around a sharp turn, leaving the motor suspended between sky and earth with nothing but space before."[5]

## ➧FROM BOOM TO BUST

By the late 1910s, several thousand cars each year rumbled through Yellowstone. During the next decade, the number of visitors skyrocketed for several reasons. First, the economy boomed during the Roaring Twenties, so more people had more money to spend on travel. Railroads also brought visitors to the park entrances, where they often joined bus tours of the park's grand loop. From 1919 to 1929, the park's annual visitation numbers jumped from 62,000 to 260,000. In 1923, the eastern area and northwest corner of the park were enlarged. Park personnel struggled to build and maintain the roads and facilities to satisfy the hordes of tourists.

Throughout the 1920s, members of Congress debated about greatly expanding Yellowstone Park. That did not happen, but in February 1929, Grand Teton National Park was established in Wyoming. After the stock market crashed in October 1929, tourism at Yellowstone decreased dramatically. Business became so bad at the park that concessionaires abandoned their facilities and left. The Great Depression lasted for most of the 1930s, and World War II followed through 1945. Yellowstone attendance lagged throughout, and the park fell into disrepair.

## ⊖ PARK ATTENDANCE THRIVES AGAIN

By the late 1940s, the tide turned again. Americans had new cars and money to spend on travel. Cross-country trips became all the rage. Railroads and tour companies seemed out-of-date to the new generation. In 1948 alone, more than 1 million people visited Yellowstone National Park. All of a sudden, the park became big business. In 1951, the Wyoming State Highway Department determined that park traffic contributed $19 million to the local economy.

Park attendance boomed during the prosperous 1950s. At the time, vacationers had few theme

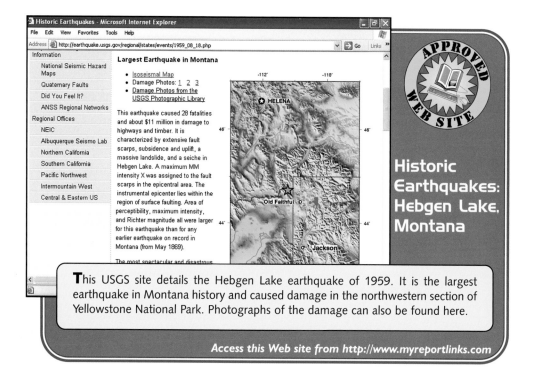

Historic Earthquakes: Hebgen Lake, Montana

This USGS site details the Hebgen Lake earthquake of 1959. It is the largest earthquake in Montana history and caused damage in the northwestern section of Yellowstone National Park. Photographs of the damage can also be found here.

*Access this Web site from http://www.myreportlinks.com*

parks or family resorts that they could visit. Instead, tourist destinations included natural wonders, with Yellowstone near the top of the list. Automobiles also improved dramatically during this decade, making trips to Yellowstone especially enjoyable. In 1955, officials launched Mission 66. This was an ambitious plan to expand Yellowstone's roads, trails, and facilities.

However, tragedy struck on August 17, 1959. A tremendous earthquake to the west of Yellowstone, occurring along the Hebgen Lake, Montana fault, created havoc in the park. Estimates put the quake at 7.5 on the Richter scale.

In a catastrophic landslide, 80 million tons of rock and timber—speeding at 170 miles per hour—roared down from a mountainside into a valley below, burying campers who were asleep in a campground. At least twenty-eight vacationers died. The debris blocked the Madison River and formed a new lake, Earthquake Lake, commonly called "Quake Lake." However, the disaster did not scare off visitors. In 1965, park attendance exceeded 2 million for the first time.

## Eco-conscious

In 1972, Yellowstone celebrated its one hundredth anniversary. Yet by this period, caretakers of the

▲ *A grizzly bear silhouetted on a mountain in Yellowstone at sunset.*

park saw it as something much more than just a "pleasuring ground" for tourists. Officials began to fully realize that human intrusion was disturbing Yellowstone's ecosystem. They did not want to discourage visitors, but they became more insistent about restoring ecological balance to the park.

For years, Yellowstone's black bears had begged tourists for food, and both grizzly and black bears had eaten out of large garbage pits. This became a major problem. Bears attacked and injured dozens of people each year, and they damaged large amounts of property. Some had to be shot because they were out of control. In 1972, Yellowstone workers removed the last of the large garbage pits, and the bears learned to eat in their natural habitats. Moreover, management strongly warned tourists to avoid coming in contact with bears.

## ⊝ ECOLOGICAL ISSUES ON THE RISE

Yellowstone faced other ecological issues in the 1960s, 1970s, and 1980s. Logging companies were allowed to cut timber in adjacent national forests, and gas and oil fields were built nearby. Both developments have altered the Greater Yellowstone Ecosystem and angered environmentalists. Within the park, officials prohibited fishing from Fishing Bridge in order to protect the spawning of the native cutthroat trout.

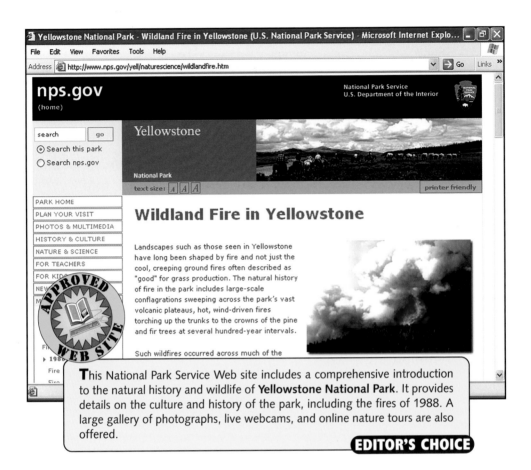

Yellowstone National Park - Wildland Fire in Yellowstone (U.S. National Park Service) - Microsoft Internet Explo...

File   Edit   View   Favorites   Tools   Help

Address 🔊 http://www.nps.gov/yell/naturescience/wildlandfire.htm          ✔ → Go   Links »

**nps.gov**
(home)

National Park Service
U.S. Department of the Interior

Yellowstone

National Park

search   go
⦿ Search this park
◯ Search nps.gov

text size: A A A                                    printer friendly

PARK HOME
PLAN YOUR VISIT
PHOTOS & MULTIMEDIA
HISTORY & CULTURE
NATURE & SCIENCE
FOR TEACHERS
FOR KIDS
NEWS
M

## Wildland Fire in Yellowstone

Landscapes such as those seen in Yellowstone
have long been shaped by fire and not just the
cool, creeping ground fires often described as
"good" for grass production. The natural history
of fire in the park includes large-scale
conflagrations sweeping across the park's vast
volcanic plateaus, hot, wind-driven fires
torching up the trunks to the crowns of the pine
and fir trees at several hundred-year intervals.

Such wildfires occurred across much of the

**T**his National Park Service Web site includes a comprehensive introduction
to the natural history and wildlife of **Yellowstone National Park**. It provides
details on the culture and history of the park, including the fires of 1988. A
large gallery of photographs, live webcams, and online nature tours are also
offered.

**EDITOR'S CHOICE**

While some corporations disrespected the need
to preserve Yellowstone, the United Nations (UN)
did not. In 1976, UNESCO, a division of the UN,
designated Yellowstone as a Biosphere Reserve.
Such reserves were created "to promote and
demonstrate a balanced relationship between
humans and the biosphere."[6] Just two years later,
UNESCO proclaimed Yellowstone a World Heritage Site. UNESCO's World Heritage Committee
considers such sites as having "outstanding uni-
versal value."[7]

## ➲ THE FIRES OF 1988

Well into the 1900s, park managers considered fires destructive, and attempted to extinguish all of them. But by mid-century, ecologists realized that forest fires (typically ignited by lightning) were a natural part of the ecosystem. In Yellowstone, for example, some of the lodgepole pines have cones that contain seeds sealed by resin. The intense heat of fire melts the resin and releases those seeds.

Realizing that controlled fires were good for Yellowstone, the park management introduced a natural fire policy in 1972. Over the next 15 years,

▲ *The fires of 1988 burned more than 793,000 of the park's acres.*

235 natural fires were allowed to burn more than 33,000 acres. The fires died out naturally. However, no one was prepared for the fires of 1988.

In late July of that year, dry conditions led to tremendous fire activity—far more than what was considered acceptable. In all, 248 fires burned in the Greater Yellowstone Ecosystem in 1988, including 50 in Yellowstone National Park. On August 20 alone, high winds spread fire over 150,000 acres. While firefighters allowed a few of the fires to rage, they tried to extinguish most of them. Twenty-five thousand firefighters were called to duty, at a cost of $120 million. But humans alone could not tame these monsters. Only the snows of November could fully douse the flames.

## → LIFE AFTER THE FIRE

In the end, 793,000 of the park's 2.2 million acres were scorched. Surprisingly, only two people died—both firefighters. The great majority of the large animals also survived. Of the park's 30,000 to 40,000 elk, only 246 were found dead.[8]

Many who watched the roaring fires on television wondered if Yellowstone would ever recover. They did not realize the ability of nature to bounce back. Scientists discovered that the animals suffered little or no effects as they resumed their normal lives. Although trees had burned

▲ *After the 1988 fires, life returned to Yellowstone faster than many had anticipated.*

down, millions and millions of seeds were also scattered across the ground. The root systems of grasses and wildflowers typically remained unharmed, and new plant growth flourished after the fires. In the years that followed, young, healthy trees rose ever higher.

Across the nation, the Yellowstone fires taught Americans valuable lessons: humans cannot control the powerful forces of nature, nor do they necessarily need to. As Ted Williams wrote in *Audubon* magazine in 1989: "Trusting nature is worth a try because trusting ourselves hasn't worked. Never have humans known enough about nature to force it to do their will."[9]

# Chapter

# 4

*Elk gather to rest at Mammoth Hot Springs.*

# Wilderness and Wildlife

In 1898, legendary nature lover John Muir was overwhelmed by the national park in Wyoming. He wrote, "A thousand Yellowstone wonders are calling, 'Look up and down and round about you!'"[1]

Indeed, natural wonders beckon from top to bottom at Yellowstone—from the majestic peaks of Mount Washburn to the floor of Canyon Country. Yellowstone is utterly unique. It is an area shaped by continental plate collisions, super-volcanic eruptions, glacial melting, and massive earthquakes. Magma looms just two miles below, with its heat seeping up to the surface. In fact, Yellowstone boasts more hot springs and geysers than the rest of the world combined. Yet in the sweet scent of a fairy slipper orchid, or the soft eyes of a snowshoe hare, Yellowstone feels like an oasis of peace and tranquility.

## ⇒A Tour of the Park

At Yellowstone, visitors can pack several vacations into one. Each area of the park is so different from the next. Let's take a tour of the land, starting in the north.

As you enter Yellow-stone's northern entrance in Montana, you are soon treated to the Mammoth Hot Springs. As heated water moves along the Morris-Mammoth Fault, it creates a "staircase" of hot spring pools, known as terraces. Temperature-sensitive algae and bacteria color these water terraces from yellow to green to orange-brown.

All of Yellowstone is at high elevation. Even the lowest points are five thousand feet above sea level. The northern section of the park to the east of Mammoth Hot Springs is a particularly high plains area. This region is characterized by its mountains, forests, expansive meadows, and broad river valleys.

Lamar Valley, noted for its glacial ponds and large boulders, rests to the northeast. This gorgeous area is nicknamed Roosevelt Country because President Theodore Roosevelt loved it so much. So do the many animals that gather there—black bears, grizzly bears, moose, elk, antelope,

The Yellowstone River passes through Hayden Valley, near the park's center.

and many others. In fact, Lamar Valley has the largest concentration of grizzlies in the entire park.

Animals also enjoy the pleasures of Hayden Valley in the center of the park, and Pelican Valley to the east. Yellowstone River cuts through Hayden Valley, a marshy area with abundant bird life. The river runs out of Yellowstone Lake. Located in southeast Wyoming, the lake basin measures twenty miles long and fourteen miles wide. While the park includes other lakes, such as the Shoshone and the Lewis, Yellowstone Lake is by far the largest.

## A VIVID DISPLAY OF COLORS

The Yellowstone River pours into the Grand Canyon of Yellowstone. This canyon has two spectacular waterfalls, the Upper and Lower Falls. The latter is 308 feet tall and enormous—more than twice the height of Niagara Falls. Stretching more than twenty miles long, the canyon is more than two thousand feet wide and a thousand feet deep. Comprised mostly of rhyolite, or volcanic rock, the canyon brims with a vivid collection of colors.

Muir described this wonder in the following words: "The walls of the cañon from top to bottom burn in a perfect glory of color, confounding and dazzling when the sun is shining—white, yellow, green, blue, vermilion, and various other shades

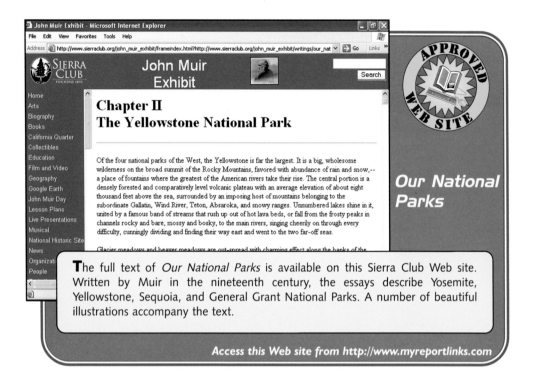

Chapter II
The Yellowstone National Park

Of the four national parks of the West, the Yellowstone is far the largest. It is a big, wholesome wilderness on the broad summit of the Rocky Mountains, favored with abundance of rain and snow,-- a place of fountains where the greatest of the American rivers take their rise. The central portion is a densely forested and comparatively level volcanic plateau with an average elevation of about eight thousand feet above the sea, surrounded by an imposing host of mountains belonging to the subordinate Gallatin, Wind River, Teton, Absaroka, and snowy ranges. Unnumbered lakes shine in it, united by a famous band of streams that rush up out of hot lava beds, or fall from the frosty peaks in channels rocky and bare, mossy and bosky, to the main rivers, singing cheerily on through every difficulty, cunningly dividing and finding their way east and went to the two far-off seas.

*Our National Parks*

**T**he full text of *Our National Parks* is available on this Sierra Club Web site. Written by Muir in the nineteenth century, the essays describe Yosemite, Yellowstone, Sequoia, and General Grant National Parks. A number of beautiful illustrations accompany the text.

*Access this Web site from http://www.myreportlinks.com*

of red indefinitely blending. All the earth here-abouts seems to be paint."[2]

## HOT WATER

Meanwhile, Yellowstone's geyser basins offer an otherworldly experience. Many of these basins dot the western section of the park. Of the approximately one thousand geysers in the world, a third are in Yellowstone.

A geyser is formed when water flows down a narrow channel in the earth. The hot rock below heats the water on the bottom, while the cool water and complicated rock fractures above act like a lid on a pressure cooker. When the water below heats to an extremely hot temperature, it can escape only by "blowing its lid" and blasting out in a violent stream. Geysers at Yellowstone can shoot thousands of gallons of water high in the sky.

Besides geysers, the park includes about ten thousand other hydrothermal features: hot springs, mud pots, and fumaroles. Yellowstone has thousands of hot springs, which are steamy, colorful pools of water. Fumaroles, the hottest hydrothermal features in Yellowstone, are basically steam vents. The emitting gas and steam create a loud hissing sound. Mud pots are acidic, mud-like hot springs. Due to their release of hydrogen sulfide, they can sometimes smell like rotten eggs.

## →Higher and Higher

A park of many dimensions, Yellowstone can be categorized by its elevation levels. The lowest areas, which are still about a mile above sea level, are prairies and riparian zones. Riparian zones are located by the banks of a river, stream, or other body of water. These areas are a favorite spot for moose. In the winter, wildlife descends from the mountains to find food here.

Above in the foothills, melting spring snow forms marshes and ponds. From a distance, the foothills seem to be blanketed by trees including

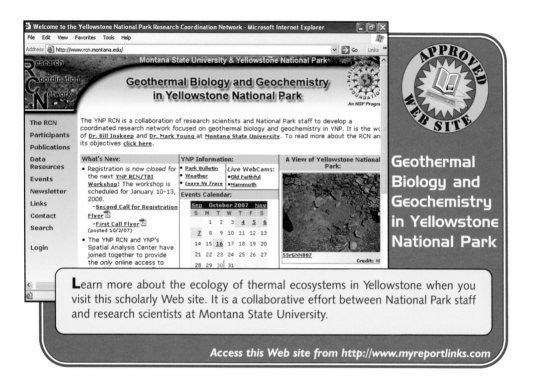

Learn more about the ecology of thermal ecosystems in Yellowstone when you visit this scholarly Web site. It is a collaborative effort between National Park staff and research scientists at Montana State University.

*Access this Web site from http://www.myreportlinks.com*

Douglas fir, pine, and aspen. But grasses, flowers and shrubs such as sagebrush also grow. Up higher, in the mountain zone, lodgepole pines dominate (these make up 80 percent of Yellowstone forests). Here and there are glorious meadows, where elk and bison graze. The highest mountain peaks are mostly lichen-covered rock, and grasses and wildflowers grow on them during the summer.

## ⊜ UNPREDICTABLE WEATHER

Yellowstone staff members can call upon a wealth of information about their park. But if you ask them what the temperature is going to be next week, you might get a blank response. As the

*The Castle Geyser at Tortoise Shell Spring.*

park's official Web site states, "unpredictability, more than anything else, characterizes Yellowstone's weather."[3]

In springtime, the temperature might reach above 70°F (21°C). Then again, during the nighttime, it could drop down to 0°F (−18°C). Yellowstone might even get a foot of spring snow. Who knows? Those who camp or hike during the spring are wise to pack both mittens and shorts, both insulated pants and suntan lotion. Of course, it becomes cooler and cooler the higher up the mountains you go.

## ⇒ LOTS OF LIGHTNING

Summers are often ideal, with daytime temperatures ranging from 70°F to about 80°F (27°C). But even in July, the nights get cold. The main concern in July and August is lightning storms, which are common. In fact, Yellowstone absorbs thousands of lightning strikes every year. When the sky crackles above, visitors are advised to leave wide-open areas, including beaches.

Autumns in Yellowstone are always chilly. The high ranges from the 40s to 60s (°F), and overnight lows dip into the teens and single digits. Even during autumn, snow begins to fall, first in the higher elevations and then below. Winters are as brutal as those in Alaska. Daytime temperatures struggle to rise above the teens and single digits, while subzero readings are typical overnight. On February 9, 1933, Yellowstone's lowest temperature ever was recorded: −66°F (−54°C)! Snow depths can vary from one to twelve feet depending on location and elevation. The deepest snow falls in the southern areas of the park.

## DIVERSE PLANT LIFE

The Greater Yellowstone Ecosystem is so diverse that it seems as if any type of plant can thrive there. In fact, the area is home to more than fifteen hundred species of plants.

Because of the chilly weather and high altitude, coniferous trees predominate in the park. The lodgepole pine is the most prevalent of the conifers, comprising at least 75 percent of Yellowstone's forests. This tree can grow more than seventy feet tall. The lodgepole pine looks like almost like a telephone pole with a Christmas tree on top. The park's other conifers include the Douglas fir, subalpine fir, whitebark pine, and Engelmann spruce. Deciduous trees, such as aspen, willow, and cottonwood, also grow in the park.

No matter the soil or terrain, flowers find a way to bloom in Yellowstone. High in the mountains at over seventy-five hundred feet, glacier lilies grow during the summer months. In drier, low-elevation areas, cacti actually grow—most notably the plains prickly pear.

▲ A field of small fringed gentian, the official flower of Yellowstone National Park. This purple flower is a common sight in geyser basins and meadows.

The Indian paintbrush, Wyoming's state flower, flourishes near the Snake River and other areas of the park. Its name comes from an American Indian legend about a brave throwing down his brushes in frustration while trying to paint a sunset. Different species of the Indian paintbrush come in different colors, including those that resemble a sunset: orange, red, yellow, and scarlet.

Bitterroot, with its pink, fingerlike petals, is Montana's state flower. American Indians used to eat this plant. But when they offered it to Meriwether Lewis (of Lewis and Clark fame), he found it "bitter and nauseous to the palate."[4] Yellowstone National Park also has its own official flower—the fringed gentian. A common sight in geyser basins and meadows, this flower features a long stem (up to three feet) and purple petals.

The yellow monkey flower and the fairy slipper are two of Yellowstone's most famous flowers. The yellow monkey flower can be found near hydrothermal features. You can't miss it, for the shape of the flower's bloom resembles a monkey's face. The fairy slipper is an orchid that grows in moist forests. Its violet flower looks like a dainty slipper.

## ⇒ABUNDANT WILDLIFE

Yellowstone is an animal lover's paradise. This park and nearby Grand Teton National Park boast the most free-roaming animals in the continental United States. Nowhere in America will you find more grizzly bears or bison.

Many types of mammals live in Yellowstone, from shrews, bats, and pikas to rabbits and weasels. But the larger hoofed mammals, as well as the bears and wolves, are what draw people by the millions to Yellowstone.

Yellowstone National Park - Microsoft Internet Explorer

File   Edit   View   Favorites   Tools   Help

Address http://www.yellowstonenationalpark.com/pages/wildlife%20fox.htm   Go   Links »

**YELLOWSTONE NATIONAL PARK.COM**

MAIN

INFORMATION

SHOP

GEOLOGY

GEYSERS

WILDLIFE

WATERFALLS

FLYFISHING

LODGING

TOURS

COMMUNITIES

CAMPING

HIKING

WILDFLOWERS

PHOT

Sixty-one different types of mammals, including the fox, make their home in the park. Learn more about **Yellowstone Wildlife** through the informative descriptions and photos of the animals on this Web site.

## ⊜ GRIZZLY AND BLACK BEARS

Grizzly bears once roamed throughout North America. Today, however, they are largely confined to only Yellowstone and Glacier national parks and the surrounding forests. These animals can weigh as much as six hundred pounds. They are omnivorous, which means that they eat both meat and plants. Because grizzlies have occasionally attacked humans, park visitors are not allowed to go within 125 yards of them.

APPROVED WEB SITE

Yellowstone Grizzlies Removed from Endangered Species List

> Yellowstone Grizzlies Removed from Endangered Species List - Microsoft Internet Explorer
>
> File  Edit  View  Favorites  Tools  Help
>
> Address http://www.sciencedaily.com/releases/2007/03/070323102911.htm  Go  Links
>
> **ScienceDaily**
> Your source for the latest research news
>
> TO VIEW TRAILER VISIT WWW.MANGA.COM OR WWW.KARAS-MOVIE.COM
>
> News | Articles | Videos | Images | Books
>
> Health & Medicine | Mind & Brain | Plants & Animals | Earth & Climate | Space & Time | Matter & Energy | Con
>
> **Science News**  Share  Blog  Cite  Science Vic
>
> **Yellowstone Grizzlies Removed from Endangered Species List**
>
> *ScienceDaily (Mar. 23, 2007)* — After nearly disappearing three decades ago, grizzly bears are thriving in the Yellowstone ecosystem and no longer need the protection of the Endangered Species Act, Deputy Interior Secretary Lynn Scarlett recently announced.
>
> See also:
>
> Plants & Animals
> • Animals
> • Ecology Research
> • Wild Animals
>
> "The grizzly's remarkable comeback is the result of years of intensive cooperative recovery efforts between federal and state agencies, conservation groups, and individuals," Scarlett said. "There is simply no way to overstate what an
>
> *On March 22, 2007, the U.S. Fish and Wildlife Service announced that the Yellowstone Distinct Population Segment of grizzly bears is a recovered population no longer meeting the ESA's definition of threatened or endangered. (Credit: National Park*
>
> ▶ Neurosurgeo Endoscopics
> ▶ Engineers D Players
> ▶ Orthopedic C Bones That (
> more scienc

**T**his article provides a short overview of grizzly bears and a look at the animals' last three decades in Yellowstone. Links to stories about other wildlife such as gray wolves, moose, and antelope are included.

*Access this Web site from http://www.myreportlinks.com*

Black bears are a little smaller than grizzlies and do not have the grizzly's distinctive shoulder hump. They are more common than grizzlies, live in the more densely forested areas, and can climb trees.

Both grizzlies and black bears are more athletic than they look. Black bears are very dangerous, and surprisingly fast: they can run at a speed of more than thirty miles per hour.

## ⊜ Elk

The elk resembles an antlered deer, only it is much more hefty and powerful. Roughly thirty thousand elk live in Yellowstone during the summer, making them the most common of the park's large hoofed mammals. During the winter, elk either remain in the park's lower elevations or migrate to areas outside the park.

The dominant male (bull) elk tries to acquire a large harem of female elk. A harem is a group of females associated with one male. The bull elk's mating sound, called bugling, punctures the air in

▲ *A bull elk makes his mating sound, called bugling.*

early autumn. As a bull elk collects his harem of cows, he considers other bulls—and humans—as potential threats. A bull elk expends a great deal of energy defending its harem from other bulls. He uses his massive antlers to engage in combat, which only rarely results in injury or death.

## ⊝ BISON

In the early 1800s, more than 60 million bison roamed the American plains. By 1894, hunters and poachers had reduced the population to only about 350 in the park. Along with a few other

Access information about a wide range of Yellowstone's wildlife at **Yellowstone National Park—Plants and Wildlife**. Details about endangered birds, bears, elk, lynx, moose, bighorn sheep, and wolf restoration efforts are all available here.

scattered herds, these were the last bison left in the United States. The bison of Yellowstone have since been protected, and today they number several thousand. These massive horned animals may seem placid, but they will gore anyone who gets too close. Many people are surprised to learn that bison are the most dangerous animals in the park.

## GRAY WOLVES

Gray wolves remain among the most talked-about animals of Yellowstone. Because people thought they killed so many animals, they were eliminated from the park in 1926. Sixty-nine years later, they were reintroduced to Yellowstone in order to prevent the overpopulation of other animals. These canines typically travel in packs, and they use their super senses of smell and hearing to attack other animals. In Yellowstone, their main prey is elk. The best chance to see the gray wolf, or to hear its impressive howl, is in Lamar Valley at dusk or dawn.

## COYOTES

Ever since Yellowstone's wolf population was restored in 1995, the coyote—a smaller canine—has struggled to compete. These canines are still a common sight, a testament to this predator's intelligence and adaptability. The coyote's high-pitched howl—a classic sound of the West—brings a smile to many a visitor.

### →MOOSE

Male moose, with their giant antlers, can weigh more than a thousand pounds. In Yellowstone, they spend much of their time near or in streams and marshes. Moose are known for their grumpy personalities. Mothers are highly protective of their young, and they'll attack predators with a swift kick of their sharp hooves.

### →MULE DEER

This species of deer is characterized by its large ears (resembling a mule's) and black-tipped tail.

Explore Yellowstone

The diverse ecosystem of Yellowstone offers a unique habitat for a large variety of wildlife. Animals profiled on this National Wildlife Federation Web site include gray wolves, mountain goats, black bears, bighorn sheep, and elk.

**EDITOR'S CHOICE**

*Access this Web site from http://www.myreportlinks.com*

It prefers living in sagebrush-grassland, where it munches on a wide variety of plants. Hunters reduced the mule deer's population in the 1800s, but it is now protected in Yellowstone.

## ⊜Bighorn Sheep and Pronghorns

A few bighorn sheep live in the mountains of Yellowstone, which they navigate with their great sense of balance and specially adapted hooves. During the breeding season, male sheep use their hard, formidable horns to ram their competitors. The pronghorn, or antelope, is found in the sage plains at the northern edge of the park, where most of the mule deer also live. With a top speed of sixty miles per hour, the pronghorn can outrun every predator in Yellowstone. It even exceeds the park's maximum speed limit!

## ⊜Strict Fishing Rules

For generations, tourists have enjoyed fishing on Yellowstone Lake and the one hundred and twenty tributaries that flow into it. Fishing Bridge, where Yellowstone River flows out of Yellowstone Lake, used to be the most popular place to cast a line. In the 1960s, close to fifty thousand people a year fished from this bridge.

Fishing in Yellowstone, however, must be regulated. Otherwise, people would deplete the waters of fish. Bald eagles, pelicans, otters, and other

A cutthroat trout, one of the park's signature fish. Fishing at Yellowstone is regulated and rules specify that if a cutthroat trout is caught, it must be thrown back into the water.

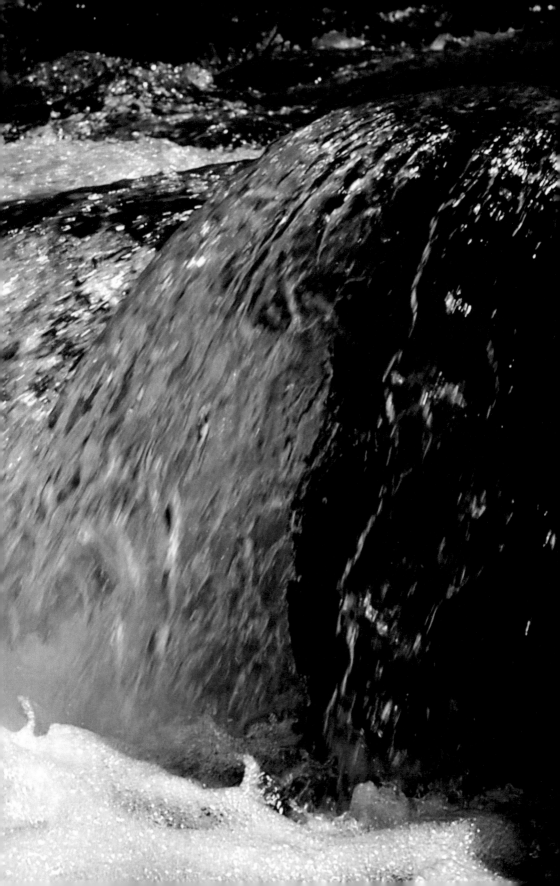

wildlife would be deprived of their food supply. Those who fish at Yellowstone must follow a strict set of rules.

## ➔ CUTTHROAT TROUT IN JEOPARDY

The cold waters of Yellowstone contain only a few native species of fish. Grayling, mountain whitefish, and cutthroat trout are the most famous. The cutthroat, the park's signature fish, earned its name due to the blood red marking below its gills. The cutthroat's population began to sharply diminish in the mid-1900s. Hundreds of millions of cutthroat eggs were shipped out of the park to fish farms. Fishermen also caught too many of the adult cutthroat trout.

In recent times, other trout have been imported to Yellowstone's waters, including the larger lake trout. An accomplished predator, the lake trout competes for food with the cutthroat and consumes many cutthroat each year, jeopardizing the population. The cutthroat trout also faces problems such as drought, which reduces their reproduction, and whirling disease, which kills their young.

Yellowstone management does not want the cutthroat population to be heavily diminished. Thus, current rules state that if you catch a cutthroat trout, you must throw it back. But if you catch a lake trout, you are required to keep it.

▲ *Trumpeter swans have pure white wings that can span seven feet. Park officials are trying to preserve this special bird.*

## ⊜MAGNIFICENT BIRDS

When it comes to Yellowstone's animals, birds are often overlooked. However, more than three hundred species of birds have been documented at the park, and some of them are mightily impressive.

More than two hundred bald eagles, America's national bird, soar above Yellowstone and Grand Teton national parks. In fact, the region is home to one of the largest concentrations of eagles in the United States. Once on the verge of extinction, the bald eagle population has stabilized. The bird is characterized by its white head and a wingspan that approaches seven feet.

The osprey looks a lot like the bald eagle, although a brown eye stripe and crooked wings distinguish it. This bird dives to lakes and streams, where it snatches slippery fish with its talons. The trumpeter swan is more timid and elegant. The "princess" of Yellowstone's birds, the trumpeter swan features pure white wings that span seven feet. Park officials are trying hard to preserve this special bird. Regulations require that visitors do not disturb it, especially when it is on its nest, because this could interfere with a swan hatching its offspring.

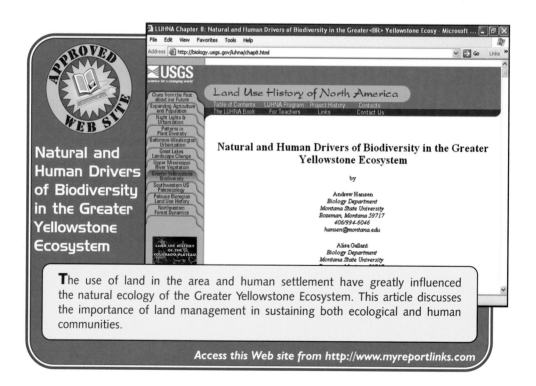

APPROVED WEB SITE

Natural and Human Drivers of Biodiversity in the Greater Yellowstone Ecosystem

LUHNA Chapter 8: Natural and Human Drivers of Biodiversity in the Greater<BR> Yellowstone Ecosy - Microsoft ...

File   Edit   View   Favorites   Tools   Help

Address   http://biology.usgs.gov/luhna/chap8.html   Go   Links

USGS
science for a changing world

Land Use History of North America

Table of Contents     LUHNA Program   Project History      Contacts
The LUHNA Book     For Teachers       Links          Contact Us

Clues from the Past about our Future
Expanding Agriculture and Population
Night Lights & Urbanization
Patterns in Plant Diversity
Baltimore-Washington Urbanization
Great Lakes Landscape Change
Upper Mississippi River Vegetation
Greater Yellowstone Biodiversity
Southwestern US Paleoecology
Palouse Bioregion Land Use History
Northeastern Forest Dynamics

LAND USE HISTORY OF THE COLORADO PLATEAU

**Natural and Human Drivers of Biodiversity in the Greater Yellowstone Ecosystem**

by

Andrew Hansen
Biology Department
Montana State University
Bozeman, Montana 59717
406/994-6046
hansen@montana.edu

Alisa Gallant
Biology Department
Montana State University

The use of land in the area and human settlement have greatly influenced the natural ecology of the Greater Yellowstone Ecosystem. This article discusses the importance of land management in sustaining both ecological and human communities.

*Access this Web site from http://www.myreportlinks.com*

## ⊜ Reptiles and Amphibians

If you're squeamish about snakes and lizards, don't worry about finding a large population of these at Yellowstone. Due to the park's cool, dry conditions, only six species of reptiles are known to live there. The wandering garter snake is the most common of these. It is largely harmless, although its bite does hurt. Do stay clear of the prairie rattlesnake, which is green and four feet long. It is the only dangerously venomous snake in the park. The sagebrush lizard, just several inches long, is the only lizard in Yellowstone.

Yellowstone's climate has limited its known amphibian species to four: the boreal toad, the chorus frog, the Columbia spotted frog, and the tiger salamander. The spotted frog is the park's most abundant amphibian. Over the years, Yellowstone's reptile and amphibian populations have declined. No one is exactly sure why. However, some blame the situation on such factors as pollution, habitat loss and fragmentation, and the importation of nonnative fish and other species.

Park management constantly strives to provide a high quality experience for tourists without impacting Yellowstone's diverse and sometimes fragile resources. Finding the right balance between meeting tourists' needs without adversely impacting the ecosystem will forever remain a daily challenge.

# Chapter

# 5

Wolves in Yellowstone have been the subject of much controversy. Wolf restoration efforts took place in 1995 to restore this predator's role in the ecosystem of the park.

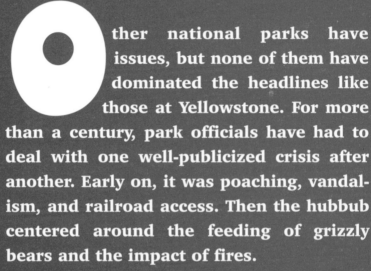

# Hot-Button Issues

Other national parks have issues, but none of them have dominated the headlines like those at Yellowstone. For more than a century, park officials have had to deal with one well-publicized crisis after another. Early on, it was poaching, vandalism, and railroad access. Then the hubbub centered around the feeding of grizzly bears and the impact of fires.

In recent years, and up to today, controversies and issues still rage. Why all the fuss? "Yellowstone was the first national park," explained Abigail Dillen, an attorney for Earthjustice (a nonprofit environmental law firm), "which makes it iconic and emotionally powerful for Americans."[1]

Recent issues have centered around Yellowstone's wolves, elk, and bison—as well as its New Zealand mud snails. And that roar you hear is not just the engines of

Yellowstone's snowmobiles, but the voices of those who oppose them.

## WOLF RESTORATION

In Yellowstone's early years, gray wolves were considered the "bad guys" of the park. They were powerful predators who killed Yellowstone's featured animals, most notably elk. Park management allowed the wolves to be killed, and they became virtually nonexistent by 1930.

In the years that followed, however, scientists realized that the wolves play an important role in

The **Greater Yellowstone Coalition**, a nonprofit founded in 1983, has pioneered the concept of ecosystem management and sustainability. A list of the threats to the Greater Yellowstone Ecosystem and the coalition's related projects, including more information about wolves in the Yellowstone area, may be found here.

the ecosystem. They had kept the ungulate, or hoofed mammal, population from growing too large, and this, in turn, affected many other plant and animal species. In 1995, amid considerable controversy, gray wolves were taken from Canada and relocated to Yellowstone.

Most local ranchers objected to the move. As wolf packs roamed out of Yellowstone, they sometimes preyed upon the ranchers' animals, including cattle and sheep. "We're in an area where a lot of game passes through and we are right in the middle of a wolf run," said Absaroka Ranch owner Budd Betts in 2000. "It's pretty much a wolf smorgasbord, and trying to make a living [while] dealing with the wolves is not fun."[2] In keeping with the Wolf Restoration Management plan, officials destroy those wolves who have preyed upon livestock. As it has turned out, wolves have done less harm to ranchers' animals than was originally feared.

## ➲ Restoring the Balance

Within Yellowstone, wolf restoration has been a great success. Wolves have helped to reduce the very large elk population, and elk carcasses have been a welcome food source for a variety of animals. Wolves' intolerance of coyotes has decreased the coyote population in and around wolf territories. This may in turn help smaller predators, rodents, and birds of prey that make up the coyotes' usual diet.

In addition, wolf watching has fascinated the park's tourists. "What a rare privilege to see wild wolves hunting, playing, and raising pups . . ." wrote frequent visitor Tim Springer. "Along with the grizzlies, the wolves are a real symbol of wilderness to me and watching them, one gets a glimpse into days gone by and the way the United States really was just a few hundred years ago."[3]

## THE NORTHERN RANGE

Elk and other ungulates love to graze on the northern range. About half of this range lies within Yellowstone National Park, and the rest lies north of its northern border in Montana. The northern range has a relatively low elevation, and it gets less snow. Thus, for the ungulates, it is the place to be during the winter months.

For more than eighty years, however, many people have worried that the northern range is overgrazed. Their concern is that all of the grazing by elk (and to a lesser extent bison) has increased erosion and led to a decline in willows, aspen, and beaver. The controversy peaked in the 1970s and 1980s. Finally, in 1986, Congress ordered a research initiative to address these concerns.

Teams of scientists found that the northern range was indeed healthy. In fact, they found that

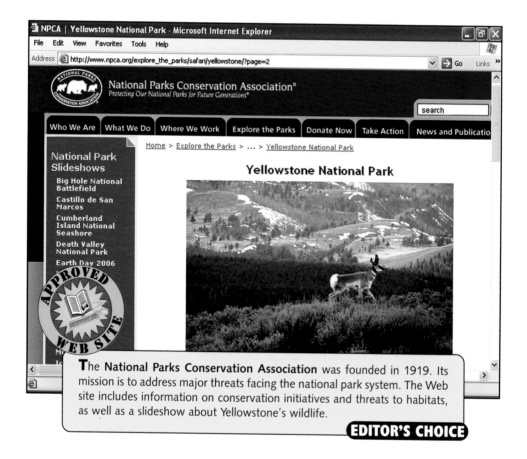

**Yellowstone National Park**

The **National Parks Conservation Association** was founded in 1919. Its mission is to address major threats facing the national park system. The Web site includes information on conservation initiatives and threats to habitats, as well as a slideshow about Yellowstone's wildlife.

**EDITOR'S CHOICE**

grazing actually enhanced grass production (except in drought years) and improved the protein content of grasses. Another report released in 2002 confirmed that the elk were not damaging the northern ranges. Nevertheless, many people still do not agree with the scientists' conclusions.

Meanwhile, the concern about the number of elk in the region has switched from thinking there were too many to a concern that there are now too few. Due primarily to wolf restoration at the park, the elk population has declined by 50 percent since 1994. But firm believers in the "circle of life" are not concerned. They believe that if the elk population drops, so too will the wolf population, since it depends on elk for food. If elk increase, the wolves will have more to eat and then will thrive. For those who have faith in the natural cycle, the northern range issue is not a concern.

## ⊜ BISON MANAGEMENT

Back in the late 1800s, most westerners lamented the slaughter of millions of bison (also known as buffalo). Hunters shot these easy targets for food, hides, money, and often just for sport. A century later, the killing of bison once again became a controversial issue. Since the early 1900s, a large percentage of Yellowstone's bison have carried an infectious disease called brucellosis, which is also carried by elk and other mammals. This disease has not had a significant effect on the park's bison. However, it has mightily scared the cattle ranchers of Montana.

For decades, many of Montana's cattle were infected with brucellosis. This was serious, since the disease could cause cattle to abort their first fetus (lose their young before they were born). It also could cause an illness called "undulant fever" in humans.

If just one cow was infected, a rancher would be forced to quarantine and perhaps destroy the entire herd. Brucellosis was disastrous for a rancher's business. Federal and state governments and the livestock industry spent hundreds of millions of dollars to eradicate, or get rid of, the disease. In 1985, Montana attained "brucellosis class-free" status.

Unfortunately for the ranchers, Yellowstone's bison are allowed to roam outside the park. At times, they graze in the same area as some of Montana's cattle. Although no bison have been

▲ Many bison in the park may carry brucellosis, an infectious disease. In this photo taken near Undine Falls, bison that have roamed out of the park are being "hazed," or herded, back into it to keep them away from livestock outside the park.

known to transmit brucellosis to livestock, a small possibility for such a transmission does exist. In 1995, the Montana Department of Livestock was allowed to capture and, if that wasn't possible, to shoot bison that roamed out of Yellowstone. In the winter of 1996–1997, they killed 1,084 bison, infuriating many Americans. "It just kills you," said Montana resident Sue Donkersgoed. "These babies [bison calves] are just not even a year old that they are massacring."[4]

In 2000, federal and Montana state officials agreed to a plan designed to better manage the issue. The plan allowed for a larger winter range for bison outside the park, although rangers and others do "haze" (or drive) bison back into the

Park Service, Montana Reach Renegade Bison Management Agreement

Fearing the spread of brucellosis from bison, cattle ranchers in Montana are urging the National Park Service to better manage the roaming animals. Learn more about it from this Web site.

Access this Web site from http://www.myreportlinks.com

park. In addition, the bison of Yellowstone would be vaccinated against the brucellosis infection. The vaccine, however, has not worked well on those bison who have been given it. Meanwhile, some bison continue to roam where they're not supposed to go. They still risk being hazed back into the park, or caught and quarantined—and even shot. In the early months of 2008, large numbers of migrating bison in search of food were shot by hunters or sent for slaughter after hazing efforts by park employees failed to keep them in the park.[5] Brucellosis will remain an issue at Yellowstone for many years to come.

## AQUATIC INVADERS

How can three little creatures—one of which is not even visible to the naked eye—cause many problems? The New Zealand mud snail may not seem intimidating, but it is one of three invaders that are threatening Yellowstone's aquatic ecosystem. None of this trio—the mud snail, a microscopic parasite, and the rainbow trout—is native to the Yellowstone region. They are nonnative, meaning they have been transported from somewhere else.

The quarter-inch-long mud snail wreaks havoc by crowding out native aquatic insect communities, which are a primary food source and habitat for small invertebrates that are food for fish. It also consumes a majority of the Yellowstone

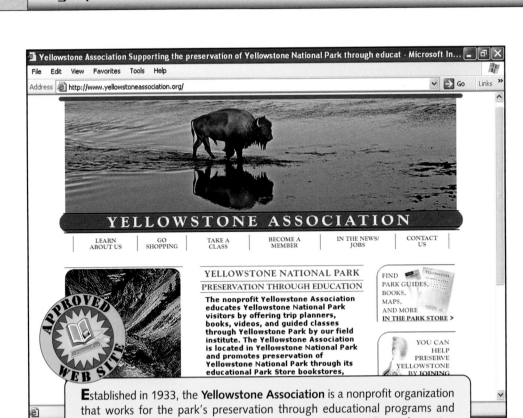

Yellowstone Association Supporting the preservation of Yellowstone National Park through educat - Microsoft In...

File   Edit   View   Favorites   Tools   Help

Address  http://www.yellowstoneassociation.org/          Go    Links

### YELLOWSTONE ASSOCIATION

| LEARN ABOUT US | GO SHOPPING | TAKE A CLASS | BECOME A MEMBER | IN THE NEWS/ JOBS | CONTACT US |

#### YELLOWSTONE NATIONAL PARK
#### PRESERVATION THROUGH EDUCATION

The nonprofit Yellowstone Association educates Yellowstone National Park visitors by offering trip planners, books, videos, and guided classes through Yellowstone Park by our field institute. The Yellowstone Association is located in Yellowstone National Park and promotes preservation of Yellowstone National Park through its educational Park Store bookstores,

FIND PARK GUIDES, BOOKS, MAPS, AND MORE
IN THE PARK STORE >

YOU CAN HELP PRESERVE YELLOWSTONE BY JOINING

APPROVED WEB SITE

Established in 1933, the **Yellowstone Association** is a nonprofit organization that works for the park's preservation through educational programs and services. News articles from its publication are here, as well as information about field courses offered through the Yellowstone Association Institute.

streams' algae growth—a primary food source for fish and other animals. Scientists are trying to develop strategies to deal with this snail.

Around 1990, an even smaller organism began to plague the area's rainbow and cutthroat trout. Since then, those species' populations have declined. A tiny parasite causes young trout to suffer from whirling disease, which damages their cartilage. This results in skeletal deformities and whirling behavior. The affected rainbow trout are unable to feed properly, which has contributed to their declining numbers. No treatment exists for the disease. To prevent other nonnative organisms from entering Yellowstone, management urges guests to clean their boats, waders, and other gear before entering the park.

In 1994, an angler caught the first verified lake trout in Yellowstone Lake. How nonnative lake trout got into Yellowstone Lake no one knows, but its initial appearance was a bad omen. The lake trout feeds on the cutthroat trout, which is native to Yellowstone's waters. Many of the area's animals depend on the cutthroat for a portion of their diet. It is estimated that each mature lake trout can consume an average of forty cutthroat per year. The cutthroat are in danger.

If no action were taken, the cutthroat population could decline by up to 60 percent during the next twenty years. Park management has tried to limit the damage by removing lake trout from Yellowstone Lake. Since lake trout control operations began over a decade ago, more than 139,000 of that species have been caught.

## UPROAR OVER SNOWMOBILES

When the first snowmobilers zoomed into Yellowstone in 1963, they didn't realize that their machines would one day cause a political firestorm. But snowmobiling at Yellowstone became more and more popular over the years, and so did the problems that came with it. In the winter of 1992–1993, more than 140,000 visitors roared along Yellowstone's powdery snow. The problems included noise and air pollution, wildlife harassment, and conflicts with other snowmobilers. Preservationists condemned the metal beasts.

Just before he left office in January 2001, President Bill Clinton ordered a phaseout of snowmobiles in Yellowstone. However, many local communities opposed the idea. People felt the end of snowmobiling would hurt the local economy.

▲ Although there is now a limited number of snowmobiles allowed in the park each day, they continue to create controversy. Here a line of snowmobiles is shown passing a group of bison on West Entrance Road.

They also didn't like being told what they could and couldn't do on public land. "It's that Manifest Destiny attitude: This is our land and we can do with it what we want," said D. J. Saunders, a policy director at the Fund for Animals.[6]

Once President George W. Bush was elected, his administration froze Clinton's decision. (Some have suggested that Vice President Dick Cheney, who is from Wyoming, pushed for the freeze.) This move angered environmentalists. Yellowstone, said Dillen of Earthjustice, "belongs to the public and the nation as a whole, not to the snowmobile industry and not to a few local business owners."[7] Then in 2003, a federal appeals court ordered the National Park Service to reinstate the phaseout. More court decisions followed, including another appeal and a restraining order against Clinton's ruling. It became a judicial mess!

Over time, park officials have worked for a compromise. On November 22, 2006, they announced plans to allow up to 720 snowmobiles in the park each day. Admissible snowmobiles would have to meet certain standards in terms of noise and pollution. Moreover, all riders would have to go with a commercial guide. Characteristically, Yellowstone officials have done their best to meet two often conflicting goals: to please tourists and to protect their park.

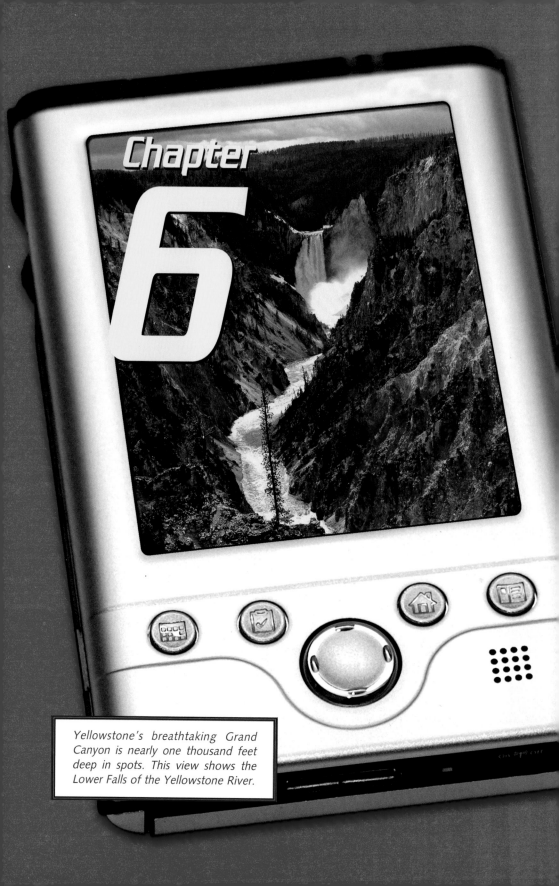

# Chapter 6

Yellowstone's breathtaking Grand Canyon is nearly one thousand feet deep in spots. This view shows the Lower Falls of the Yellowstone River.

# Endless Adventures

**E**ach year, hundreds of thousands of Americans explore the magic of Yellowstone for the first time. Others, such as George Nikitin of San Francisco, return over and over. "I can't imagine a more beautiful, spectacular, and soulful place to be," Nikitin said.[1]

Unless you live in the surrounding area, it is not easy to get to Yellowstone. The nearby airports—such as those in Jackson Hole, Wyoming, and Bozeman, Montana—are small, and the airfares are high. The park is also hundreds of miles away from a major metropolitan area. Thus, it takes most people hours or days to drive there. Nevertheless, people from all over North America make the trip. "My kids liked to keep a list of all the different license plates they saw . . . to see how far people came from to go to Yellowstone," wrote Joan Shott. "The list was extensive. [W]e counted over forty states and half a dozen Canadian provinces."[2]

Though Yellowstone may be difficult to get to, the entrance fees are not expensive. Just $25 will pay for a carload of tourists to pass through the gates, and those arriving on bike or foot are admitted for just $12. The entrance permit allows the visitor to come and go into both Yellowstone and Grand Teton National Park for seven days. Visitors can explore Yellowstone on their own or pay for one of many tours. Park rangers recommend

YellowstonePark.com is a trip planning resource that will help you learn more about the world's oldest national park. Interactive maps, information on the wildlife, and featured regions to explore are highlights, along with a list of the top ten things to see in Yellowstone. Photographs and podcasts are also featured.

that vacationers stay at least three days to fully experience Yellowstone's natural delights and attend some of the many free programs provided by park staff.

## → WHAT TO SEE

When visitors enter Yellowstone for the first time, they typically ask the same questions: "What are the main attractions, and which ones should we see first?" Yellowstone.net provides newcomers with a "must see" list of popular sites within the park.[3] First on the list is no surprise:

- **Old Faithful Geyser and Upper Geyser Basin**

Thanks to its reliability and spectacular display, Old Faithful is the most popular attraction in the park. Every hour to an hour and a half, without fail, Old Faithful erupts. Onlookers are amazed by the sight of four to eight thousand gallons of boiling water blasting into the air. The geyser shoots more than one hundred feet up, and its eruptions last from one and a half to five minutes.

Visitors can stroll around the Upper Geyser Basin and see other famous geysers, including Grotto, Castle, and Daisy, and many beautiful hot spring pools. Morning Glory Pool, about a mile and a half from Old Faithful, is the size of a backyard swimming pool. Its colors are amazingly vibrant. Surrounding the sky-blue pool are rings of green, yellow, orange, and red that change color depending on water conditions.

• **Grand Canyon of the Yellowstone**

Scientists are not really sure how Yellowstone's Grand Canyon was formed. Like everyone else, they are content to stand back and enjoy the awesome views. The Grand Canyon plunges a thousand feet deep, exposing rock made up of iron compounds. The oxidizing (or rusting) of the iron gives the canyon its yellow and copper hues.

From such spots along the canyon's rim as Artist Point and South Rim Trail, tourists can view the Lower Falls waterfall in all its glory. Up to 60,000 gallons of water per second plunges 308 feet. The canyon's Upper Falls and Crystal Falls are also "must sees."

◄ A view of the Lower Falls waterfall in Yellowstone's Grand Canyon.

### • Hayden Valley

Hayden Valley is the place to go to experience Yellowstone's magnificent wildlife. It is one of the best locations in America to see herds of bison roaming the plains. Elk and coyote are also plentiful, and you might even see a grizzly bear. The Yellowstone River cuts through Hayden Valley, attracting ducks, geese, pelicans, and the occasional bald eagle.

### • Mammoth Hot Springs

At this popular site, hot and colorful water cascades down massive terraces. The color is purely natural and is caused by the different kinds of living bacteria in the water. These bacteria create ever-changing shades of oranges, yellows, greens, pinks, and browns.

The Mammoth Hot Springs' Lower Terraces feature such formations as the Liberty Cap (a thirty-seven-foot hot spring cone) and the Palette Spring (a spring resembling a painter's palette). The Mammoth's Upper Terrace Loop features the Canary Spring, named for its stunning canary-yellow color.

### • Yellowstone Lake

Yellowstone Lake is unlike any other in the United States. It is immense, measuring 136 square miles in area, and it is 7,733 feet above sea level. This makes it the largest freshwater lake in the United States at such a high altitude,

▲ Ice thaws on the immense Yellowstone Lake, surrounded by snow-capped mountains.

and the second largest in the world at that altitude. The surrounding mountains, often capped with snow, make the visit to the lake a truly unique experience.

Because of Yellowstone Lake's large size and depth, strong winds can create ocean-like waves. When it is not frozen solid, the water is always cold. Park officials strongly advise against swimming in the lake, even in the middle of summer.

Trout fishing there, however, can be a delightful experience. Perhaps the best way to enjoy Yellowstone Lake is to lounge on the porch of Lake Lodge, soaking in the sights and sounds.

### • Norris Geyser Basin

If you're feeling a bit chilly, head on over to Norris Geyser Basin. It is the hottest hydrothermal area in Yellowstone, with a top recorded temperature of 459°F. In addition, this basin is considered the most diverse and unpredictable area in the world. Steam vents evolve into hot springs, and pools can develop into geysers.

The park provides several miles of boardwalks for tourists to enjoy the hydrothermal features. Both the Emerald and Green Dragon springs are characterized by their steaming green water. The geysers, though, are the main attraction. Steamboat is the world's tallest active geyser. In eruptions that last from three to forty minutes, it shoots water up to three hundred feet into the air. Unfortunately, eruptions of Steamboat are very unpredictable and tend to be rare. It erupted three times in 2003, and not at all in 2004.

The Echinus geyser, however, usually erupts one to two times every day. Its pools slowly fill with water, then blast steam and water up to sixty feet skyward. Echinus is the largest known acid-water geyser in the world. Its water is as acidic as vinegar.

### • Lamar Valley

Lamar Valley is remotely located in the park's northeastern area. But for those who are determined to view wildlife, it is worth the trip. The large valley is home to bison, elk, pronghorn, moose, and coyote, as well as a large concentration of grizzly bears. Wolf packs also roam the valley, especially at dawn and dusk. Osprey and bald eagles fly above. In the spring, Lamar Valley offers a rare and unforgettable sight: baby bison and elk exploring their new world.

### • Tower Fall

Outside of the Grand Canyon of Yellowstone, Tower Fall is the most beloved waterfall in the park. When Thomas Moran unveiled his painting of Tower Fall in 1872, it spurred Congress to preserve Yellowstone as a national park.

Tower Fall, in the north-central part of the park, is the waterfall of Tower Creek. Framed by eroded volcanic pinnacles, the water plummets 132 feet. Visitors can hike down to the bottom of the canyon to witness the spectacle. During the winter, the entire waterfall is encased in ice.

### • Lower Geyser Basin/Fountain Paint Pots

The Lower Geyser Basin offers a wide variety of hydrothermal features for tourists to enjoy. Covering nearly twelve square miles, the basin includes geysers, mud pots, pools, springs, and fumaroles. The area's Great Fountain geyser rivals

Old Faithful, spouting water one hundred fifty feet high. White Dome geyser shoots water out of a dome-shaped white rock. When it erupts, it looks like a mini-volcano.

Fountain Paint Pots are mud pots composed of clay and silica. They seem to be painted in red, brown, and yellow. In the spring and early summer, the mud is thin, and steam and gases bubble to the surface. Visitors may think they're on the set of a science-fiction movie, but the Fountain Paint Pots are just another of Yellowstone's many wonders.

### • West Thumb Geyser Basin

West Thumb is one of Yellowstone's smaller basins. However, it offers the full range of hydrothermal features—from geysers to fumaroles. The basin is located along the west "thumb" of Yellowstone Lake. In fact, some of the hydrothermal features are even in the lake. Fishing Cone is one such feature. This rock, located a few feet off shore, is shaped like a circular sci-fi spaceship. The top of the vent is only three feet above the level of the water. Years ago, anglers would catch fish while standing on the rock and then parboil them in the vent.

## ⇒ GET ACTIVE

Not just for viewing, Yellowstone is a great place for doing. The park offers almost every outdoor

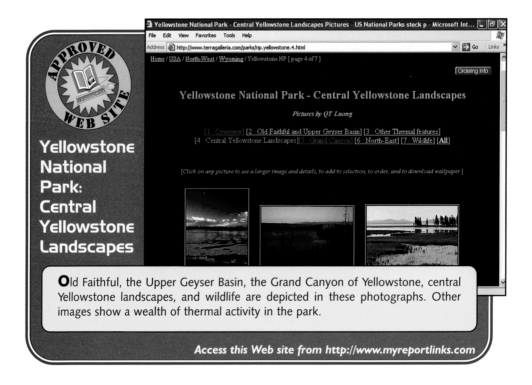

Yellowstone
National
Park:
Central
Yellowstone
Landscapes

Old Faithful, the Upper Geyser Basin, the Grand Canyon of Yellowstone, central Yellowstone landscapes, and wildlife are depicted in these photographs. Other images show a wealth of thermal activity in the park.

Access this Web site from http://www.myreportlinks.com

activity imaginable, from camping and fishing to hiking and biking. Before visitors go exploring, they must remember: safety first. Hundreds of people have died in Yellowstone since it was declared a national park. Explorers should stay on designated safe trails to avoid falling into boiling liquids or inhaling toxic gas. They should dress for the weather, take proper supplies, and avoid exploring alone. Visitors must take care not to approach dangerous animals and should read relevant literature, including the Bear Management Guidelines. Finally, guests should listen to the park rangers and always pay attention to the signs.

## →CAMPING UNDER THE STARS

Though visually stunning during the day, Yellowstone is just as magnificent at night. "When you look up to the sky and see that canopy of stars overhead, it's just . . . amazing," said Elizabeth Alvarez, who supports limiting artificial lights in Yellowstone.[4]

At Yellowstone, sleeping beneath the stars can be a heavenly experience—as long as the weather is nice. The park's campsites fill up in July and August, but the nighttime temperatures in the other months are just too low. Even in the heart of summer, campers need to bring heavy sleeping bags. In addition, tents need to be dependable enough to protect campers from high winds and thunderstorms.

Yellowstone features twelve campgrounds. The largest areas are Bridge Bay, Canyon, Fishing Bridge RV, Grant Village, and Madison. These are the only Yellowstone campgrounds that accept reservations. The park's campgrounds offer a wide range of experiences: the largest are equipped with showers, laundry facilities, and flush toilets. But many of the smaller campgrounds have no showers, and only have vault toilets (no running water) and rustic water pumps.

Campers need to be careful to put away their food, dishes, and utensils after eating—or risk having bears for guests. The park's rangers strictly enforce this rule to protect the safety of the campers and the bears. A bear that consumes human food will often have to be killed because of the danger it creates for campers.

## ➡ ENDLESS TRAILS FOR HIKING

Yellowstone offers more than 2 million acres for exploration, including 1,300 miles of trails. However, most of the park is undeveloped wilderness. The park's animals are unpredictable, as is the weather. Streams can be turbulent, lakes frigid, and hydrothermal features scalding hot. Those who hike in the mountains risk stepping on loose rock. As the National Park Service's official Web site warns, "If you choose to explore and

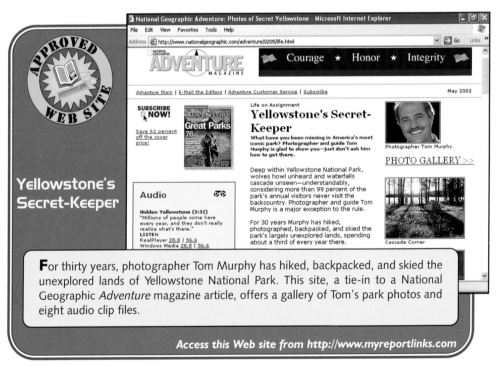

**Yellowstone's Secret-Keeper**

For thirty years, photographer Tom Murphy has hiked, backpacked, and skied the unexplored lands of Yellowstone National Park. This site, a tie-in to a National Geographic *Adventure* magazine article, offers a gallery of Tom's park photos and eight audio clip files.

*Access this Web site from http://www.myreportlinks.com*

enjoy the natural wonders of Yellowstone, there is no guarantee of your safety. Be prepared for any situation."[5]

Before beginning a hike, guests should enter a visitor center or ranger station for information. They provide backcountry regulations and guidelines as well as updated news about trail conditions, including weather or bear activity in the area. Hikers should bring along their own water because the water from lakes and streams may not be safe to drink. Proper clothing, a cell phone, a first-aid kit, insect repellent, and sunscreen are also recommended. It is important that hikers not venture into the wilderness on their own. Permits are required for the backcountry camps.

## ⊝ WATER SPORTS

When the weather is warm and pleasant, nothing can match a boat ride in Yellowstone. However, the park strictly regulates which waters and vessels tourists can use. First of all, every boater needs to purchase a permit, even for nonmotorized boats. Boating is prohibited on all of Yellowstone's rivers and streams, although hand-propelled boats are allowed on the Lewis River Channel.

Yellowstone Lake and Lewis Lake have the fewest restrictions. On these waters, visitors can ride in canoes, kayaks, and motor boats, all of which are available for rental. But even on the lakes, canoeists and kayakers need to stay close to shore. Strong winds can capsize their boats, and the water is too cold for swimming.

## ➔ BIKING THROUGH PARADISE

What could be more serene than a bike ride through paradise? Under the right conditions, cycling in Yellowstone can be a glorious experience. But riders face numerous restrictions. Yellowstone's main roads are not biker-friendly. They are narrow and curvy, and don't have any bike lanes. RVs take up the entire right lane. The mountainous climbs can be strenuous, and spring and fall weather (rain, sleet, and snow) can be perilous.

At Yellowstone, bicycles are not allowed on park trails and in backcountry areas. The rules also require bikes to have a red light or reflector on the rear and a white light on the front. Despite the limitations, many routes are made available to bicyclists—three hundred miles all told. If you follow the rules and find the route that's right for you, you could be in for the best ride of your life. Bicyclists recommend the spring and fall for the best experience: fewer cars, abundant campsites, and cool weather make for better conditions.

## ➔ REEL 'EM IN

Every year, tens of thousands of anglers make a pilgrimage to Yellowstone. "[Y]ou can go to other places in the world and catch bigger fish," said Arrick Swanson, "but you're not going to get them on a dry fly."[6]

The park offers fishing options at 220 lakes and 2,650 miles of rivers and streams. Traditionally, the Yellowstone River below Yellowstone Lake and the Firehole and Madison rivers have been the top spots to drop a line. For those anglers who are willing to take a short hike, the park offers hundreds of good lakes and streams.

Because of the huge numbers of anglers, Yellowstone officials have had to enact strict regulations. Those aged fifteen and older need to purchase a fishing permit. Fishing sites have opening and closing dates—roughly June through October. Only nontoxic tackle (no lead) is permitted. Since 2001, all native sport fish species in Yellowstone have been subject to catch-and-release-only fishing rules. Such fish include the cutthroat trout and its subspecies as well as the mountain whitefish and the Montana grayling.

Despite the limitations, Yellowstone keeps luring anglers back for more. "It's like a ritual," said Jerry Wiese of Colorado. "The park is beautiful and relaxing, and the fishing is very good."[7]

## GIDDY-UP!

At Yellowstone, even a horse-riding novice can feel like an Old West cowboy or cowgirl. Xanterra

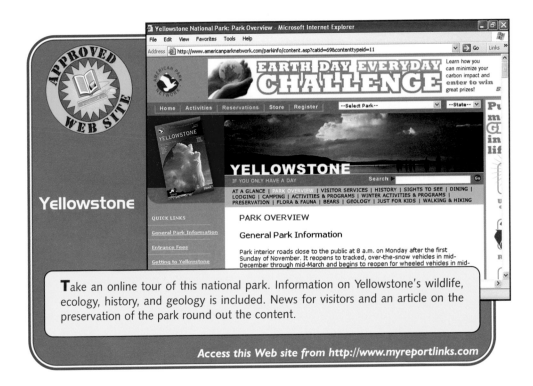

Take an online tour of this national park. Information on Yellowstone's wildlife, ecology, history, and geology is included. News for visitors and an article on the preservation of the park round out the content.

**Access this Web site from http://www.myreportlinks.com**

Parks & Resorts offers slow, gentle horse ride tours of one or two hours in length. Riders are led on scenic tours at Mammoth Hot Springs, or through the Roosevelt Lodge and Lamar Valley areas. For experienced riders, area outfitters and dude ranches offer more adventurous tours. Visitors are even allowed to bring their own horses into the park, though restrictions apply.

## A GREAT PLACE FOR A PICNIC

Yellowstone has plenty of restaurants, but who wants to eat inside? The park offers more than forty picnic areas, most near major roadways. Picnicking near Yellowstone Lake has always been popular. Others enjoy a homemade lunch at Lava Creek, just upstream from Undine Falls. The Canyon picnic area, near Artist Point at the Grand Canyon, is another favorite. Fires are permitted only at picnic areas that have fire grates, and none of the areas have running water. To prevent visits by animals, you must clean up your food and garbage.

## ⮞ WHERE TO STAY

Most of Yellowstone's 3 million annual visitors do not want to camp under the stars. Fortunately, they have plenty of options for lodging. Tourists can stay in rustic cabins, inexpensive motels, or elegant hotels.

Many visitors prefer to stay in Yellowstone's surrounding "gateway communities." Most of these are close to the park's entrances — Gardiner, Red Lodge, and West Yellowstone, Montana. Others are located in Wyoming, including Jackson Hole and Cody.

Many tourists are hesitant about staying inside the park because of the lack of amenities. Some of the inns have been around for roughly a century. Moreover, park officials try to keep technology to a minimum. Very few rooms have televisions, and many do not have phones or Internet connections. Some cabins do not even have heat, only wood-burning stoves. Visitors are encouraged to take evening walks and attend naturalist talks. The lobbies of many of the lodges are architectural gems and the perfect place to play cards, board games, visit with others, or read a book—just as visitors have done for more than one hundred years.

Tourists love the old inns and hotels. Old Faithful Inn, next to the famous geyser, is the most popular lodging facility in the park. Established in 1904, the inn is rustic style with a log and wood exterior. The huge lobby includes an enormous stone fireplace.

The Lake Yellowstone Hotel has been a favorite since 1891. Painted in cheery yellow, it oversees the park's signature lake. The hotel has a 1920s feel, although it was beautifully renovated around 1990. Its restaurant is elegant, and the views are spectacular—especially from the Sun Room.

## ➔ WHAT TO EAT

When it comes to food, Yellowstone caters to everyone from the well-to-do to those on a tight budget. Visitors can dine on prime rib at a hotel restaurant or grab a sandwich at the Pony Express deli. Most of the park's eateries are casual. The Lake, Old Faithful, and Canyon lodges feature popular cafeterias. Other areas include delicatessens, snack shops, and soda fountains.

For a once-in-a-lifetime experience, visitors should consider the Old West Dinner Cookout. The dinner is held in Pleasant Valley, about three miles from Roosevelt Lodge. Covered wagons and horses carry guests from the Roosevelt Corral to the cookout. Dinner is served on picnic tables with protection overhead, and often a singing cowboy provides entertainment. The buffet-style meal includes steak, chuck wagon corn, potato salad, cole slaw, baked beans, corn muffins, and watermelon. Now that's good eatin'!

## → Visitor Centers and Museums

Yellowstone's eight visitor and information centers help newcomers to get acquainted with the park and its history. The five major centers include the Albright, Old Faithful, Canyon, Fishing Bridge, and Grant Village.

The Albright Visitor Center and Museum, located in Mammoth Hot Springs, is open year-round. It includes a historical museum that profiles the region's American Indians and early explorers. Park rangers also show short films, such as *The Challenge of Yellowstone*. At the Old Faithful Visitor Center, a visitor education center is in the works. Its exhibits and interactive media will focus on Yellowstone's hydrothermal features. The Yellowstone Park Foundation has raised millions of dollars for this state-of-the-art project.

## ⊖WINTER WONDERLAND

At Yellowstone, winter means more than just the three-month season denoted on the calendar. The park's "winter" period stretches from early November to mid-April—nearly half the year. Sections of the park do remain open during these months, and visitors are welcome.

Most of Yellowstone's roads are closed during the winter, although State Road 212 remains open. Fortunately, tourists can drive through Lamar Valley, which is a great place for wolf watching during the winter. Sightseers can also visit Mammoth Hot Springs and its museum. Some businesses offer snowcoach tours. These

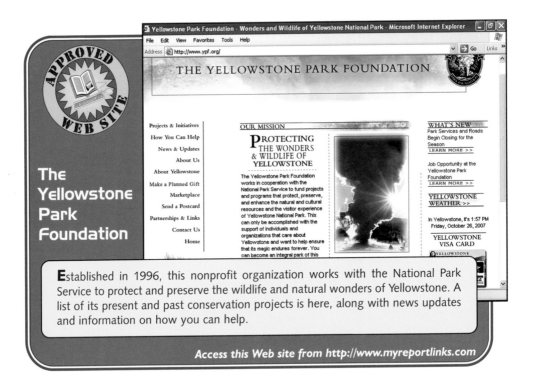

The Yellowstone Park Foundation

Established in 1996, this nonprofit organization works with the National Park Service to protect and preserve the wildlife and natural wonders of Yellowstone. A list of its present and past conservation projects is here, along with news updates and information on how you can help.

*Access this Web site from http://www.myreportlinks.com*

large vehicles are especially made to drive on snow without getting stuck. Visitors can stop by various warming huts for a snack and hot chocolate. These huts are located along the roads used by snowmobiles and snowcoaches.

Many wintertime enthusiasts go to Yellowstone to play. Each year, thousands of snowmobilers roar into the park to enjoy the fresh snow and wide-open spaces. As discussed in Chapter 5, snowmobilers must adhere to strict regulations. Cross-country skiing is another favorite pastime in the area. In fact, the training area for the U.S. Olympic cross-country ski teams is located in the town of West Yellowstone.

The National Park Service maintains and rates numerous cross-country ski trails in Yellowstone. The Biscuit Basin Loop is rated "easiest." This five-mile trail, which passes many hydrothermal features, has an elevation change of only forty feet. Mallard Creek Loop, a twelve-mile trail, is dubbed "more difficult to most difficult." The elevation change is 760 feet, and at times it is steep with difficult turns.

## ➔ Precautions a Must

Skiers and all wintertime visitors must take supreme precautions. Dangers are everywhere. Skiers can get lost in a sea of white, especially during a blizzard. Winds are often ferocious, and temperatures can plunge far below zero. The ground around hydrothermal features can be unstable, with hot water bubbling beneath sheets of ice. Skiers should watch for signs of hypothermia and frostbite. They also should dress properly for the bitter cold and bring supplies such as a compass, map, and whistle. The best advice of all: always stick with a group or a partner.

## NEARBY ATTRACTIONS

Grand Teton National Park is located just south of Yellowstone. At 310,000 acres, it is smaller than its famous sister park, yet still attracts more than 3 million visitors a year. Grand Teton lacks Yellowstone's amazing hydrothermal features, but it does offer one thing Yellowstone does not: views of the spectacular Teton mountain range.

This range is the park's central feature. It includes eight peaks that exceed 12,000 feet, including the Grand Teton at 13,770 feet. The park also boasts more than a hundred alpine lakes as well as a variety of wildlife similar to Yellowstone's. Popular attractions include the Jenny Lake Scenic Drive and the Signal Mountain Summit Road. Menor's Ferry carries visitors across the Snake River. Visitors can also take guided raft trips on the Snake River.

Tourists could spend the entire summer exploring Yellowstone's surrounding area. Yellowstone and Grand Teton are literally engulfed by national forests, all of which are open to the public. The Beartooth Highway winds through the Beartooth Plateau and mountains of the Custer, Shoshone, and Gallatin national forests. It ranks among the top scenic drives in America.

The towns nearest to Yellowstone still have the spirit and charm of the Old West. They include the Montana towns of West Yellowstone, Red Lodge, and Gardiner. Cody, Wyoming, is home to a nightly rodeo and the Buffalo Bill Museum. Jackson, Wyoming, is situated in the Jackson Hole valley, just south of Grand Teton National Park. Jackson Hole Mountain Resort is considered one of the best ski areas in North America.

## An Experience of a Lifetime

In 2006, the National Parks Traveler Web site asked users to pick their favorite national park in the United States. Yellowstone was the hands-down winner. For parts of three centuries, tens of millions of visitors have enjoyed Yellowstone's awe-inspiring waterfalls, geysers, wildlife, and more. "If [sightseeing] is all you can do, it is worth it," wrote Yellowstone lover Thomas Bream, "but if at all possible, get into the park and experience it. You won't be disappointed. It is as beautiful as America gets."[8]

## Report Links

The Internet sites described below can be accessed at
http://www.myreportlinks.com

▶**Yellowstone National Park**
**Editor's Choice** This National Park Service Web site provides a very good overview of the park.

▶**Yellowstone: America's Sacred Wilderness**
**Editor's Choice** PBS offers a glimpse into the natural history of Yellowstone.

▶**Explore Yellowstone**
**Editor's Choice** Learn more about the wildlife in Yellowstone National Park.

▶**Yellowstone, the First National Park**
**Editor's Choice** Learn about the establishment of Yellowstone National Park.

▶**National Parks Conservation Association**
**Editor's Choice** This environmental nonprofit works to protect and preserve America's national parks.

▶**Windows Into Wonderland: Yellowstone National Park**
**Editor's Choice** Take an electronic field trip to Yellowstone Park.

▶**The Evolution of the Conservation Movement, 1850–1920**
This historical collection includes photos and manuscripts related to conserving our national heritage.

▶**Geology Fieldnotes: Yellowstone National Park**
Find out about the geological formation and evolution of Yellowstone National Park.

▶**Geothermal Biology and Geochemistry in Yellowstone National Park**
This publication is a compilation of information gathered at a geological workshop.

▶**Greater Yellowstone Coalition**
Preservation of the Greater Yellowstone region is the mission of this environmental group.

▶**Historic Earthquakes: Hebgen Lake, Montana**
Learn about a 1959 earthquake that caused damage in Yellowstone National Park.

▶**Journal of a Trapper**
Read this firsthand account of a nineteenth-century adventurer's expedition to Yellowstone.

▶**Lewis and Clark**
Visit this PBS site to learn more about Lewis and Clark.

▶**Natural and Human Drivers of Biodiversity in the Greater Yellowstone Ecosystem**
Scientists from Montana State University explore the Greater Yellowstone Ecosystem.

▶*Our National Parks*
A collection of ten essays by naturalist John Muir.

## Report Links

### The Internet sites described below can be accessed at http://www.myreportlinks.com

▶**Park Service, Montana Reach Renegade Bison Management Agreement**
This article discusses bison management in Yellowstone.

▶**The Shoshone Indians**
The history and culture of the Shoshone Indian tribe can be found on this site.

▶**U.S. National Parks & Monuments Travel Guide: Yellowstone National Park**
For a good overview of the geology and wildlife of the park, visit this site.

▶**Volcano Monitoring at Yellowstone National Park**
Volcano monitoring at Yellowstone National Park is examined on this Web site.

▶**Yellowstone**
This is a comprehensive information guide to Yellowstone National Park.

▶**Yellowstone Association**
This nonprofit is interested in conserving the national park through its educational efforts.

▶**Yellowstone Grizzlies Removed from Endangered Species List**
*Science Daily* looks at the grizzly bear comeback in Yellowstone.

▶**Yellowstone Historical Almanac**
Find historical documents about Yellowstone on these Web pages.

▶**Yellowstone National Park: Central Yellowstone Landscapes**
For photographs of Yellowstone National Park, visit this online gallery.

▶*Yellowstone National Park: Its Exploration and Establishment*
Learn more about Yellowstone when you read this online history book.

▶**Yellowstone National Park—Plants and Wildlife**
The plants and wildlife of Yellowstone are the subject of these Web pages.

▶**YellowstonePark.com**
Resources that will help you plan a trip to the park are available on this site.

▶**The Yellowstone Park Foundation**
Working with the NPS, this nonprofit has the long-term conservation of the park as its mission.

▶**Yellowstone's Secret-Keeper**
A *National Geographic* photographer shares pictures of Yellowstone.

▶**Yellowstone Wildlife**
Meet the animals of Yellowstone through descriptions and photos.

**alpine**—Refers to a high mountain area where cold temperatures and wind exposure keep trees from growing.

**basin**—A geographical area drained by a river and its tributaries.

**biosphere**—The part of the earth, including air, water, and land, in which life exists.

**caldera**—A giant bowl-like depression in the earth's surface caused when a magma chamber collapses following a rapid, massive volcanic eruption.

**coniferous**—A plant that bears cones.

**deciduous**—A plant that loses its leaves every autumn.

**ecosystem**—A community of organisms that interact with one another. The ecosystem includes the environment in which the organisms live.

**environmentalist**—A person who strives to protect the environment from pollution or destruction.

**expedition**—A journey by a group of people that is organized for a particular purpose.

**fumarole**—A vent on the earth's surface that emits hot gas and water vapor.

**geyser**—A hot spring that erupts water and steam.

**gorge**—A narrow, steep-sided canyon or valley.

**Greater Yellowstone Ecosystem**—The only large, nearly intact ecosystem in the earth's northern temperate zone. It encompasses Yellowstone National Park and its surrounding area.

**hot spring**—A pool that has formed from hot water seeping to the earth's surface.

**hydrothermal**—Pertains to water that was heated beneath the earth's surface by magma.

**hypothermia**—A condition in which one's body temperature becomes dangerously low.

**ice ages**—From one million to twelve thousand years ago, when enormous ice sheets covered much of North America.

**ironic**—Symbolic or representative of.

**magma**—Melted rock beneath the earth's surface.

**mountain men**—Trappers (mainly of beaver fur) and explorers who worked in the Rocky Mountain area in the early to mid-1800s.

**mud pot**—A pool of hot water and fine sediment through which steam, water, and volcanic gas escape.

**petrified**—Plant material that has been replaced by rock.

**plains**—A vast area of flat land.

**poacher**—One who hunts or fishes illegally.

**predator**—An animal that seizes, kills, and eats other animals.

**preservationist**—A person who advocates protecting a natural environment with minimal human intervention.

**rhyolite**—Light-colored volcanic rock.

**squatter**—Someone who settles on land without the legal right to do so.

**super volcano**—A volcano that produces exceptionally large eruptions, often resulting in a caldera.

**tectonic plates**—Large, movable pieces of earth that lie deep underground.

**ungulates**—Hoofed mammals.

**vermillion**—Bright red pigment.

## Chapter 1. Wonderland

1. Steve Watson, interview by author, e-mail, October 20, 2006.

2. Ibid.

3. Ibid.

4. "Forest Resources and Environmental Science," *Michigan Tech,* n.d., <http://forest.mtu.edu/classes/fw4500/index.html> (January 3, 2007).

5. Ibid.

## Chapter 2. Evolution and Exploration

1. Paul Schullery, *Searching for Yellowstone: Ecology and Wonder in the Last Wilderness* (New York: Houghton Mifflin Company, 1997), p. 52.

2. Ibid., p. 25.

3. Ibid., p. 30.

4. Ibid., p. 36.

5. Hiram Martin Chittenden, *The Yellowstone National Park* (Norman, Okla.: University of Oklahoma Press, 1964), p. 40.

6. Marjorie Benson, *Wonders of the World: Yellowstone* (Austin, Tex.: Raintree Steck-Vaughn Publishers, 1995), p. 17.

7. "'Peetrified' Resources: fossils and human culture," *Rosetta Stones,* May 23, 2006, <http://rosettastone.wordpress.com/2006/05/23/peetrified-resources-fossils-and-human-culture/> (January 3, 2007).

8. Chittenden, p. 48.

9. Benson, p. 18.

10. Schullery, p. 55.

11. Benson, p. 6.

12. "Yellowstone: First National Park," yellowstoneparknet.com, n.d., <http://www.yellowstoneparknet.com/history/first_national_park.php> (January 3, 2007).

## Chapter 3. A History of the Park

1. Paul Schullery, *Searching for Yellowstone: Ecology and Wonder in the Last Wilderness* (New York: Houghton Mifflin Company, 1997), p. 72.

2. Seabring Davis and Brian Hurlbut, *Insiders' Guide to Yellowstone and Grand Teton* (Guilford, Conn.: The Globe Pequot Press, 2003), p. 21.

3. "Historic Yellowstone Photos From Wyoming Tales and Trails," *Wyoming Tales and Trails,* n.d., <http://www.wyomingtalesandtrails.com/yellowstoneb.html> (January 3, 2007).

4. Historic Roads in the National Park System, "The Development of Park Roads," *National Park Service,* August 23, 2004, <http://www.cr.nps.gov/history/online_books/roads/shs2.htm> (January 3, 2007).

5. Ibid.

6. People, Biodiversity, and Ecology, "Statutory Framework for the World Network of Biosphere Reserves," *UNESCO,* n.d., <http://www.unesco.org/mab/ecosyst/urban/doc.shtml> (January 3, 2007).

7. "World Heritage site," *Encyclopedia Britannica Online,* n.d., <http://www.britannica.com/eb/article-9077491/World-Heritage-site> (January 3, 2007).

8. F. J. Singer, W. Schreier, J. Oppenheim and E. O. Garton, "Drought, Fire and Large Mammals," *Bioscience,* Vol. 39, 1989, pp. 716–722.

9. Marjorie Benson, *Wonders of the World: Yellowstone* (Austin, Tex.: Raintree Steck-Vaughn Publishers, 1995), Benson, p. 47.

## Chapter 4. Wilderness and Wildlife

1. John William Uhler, "The Total Yellowstone Page," yellowstone-natl-park.com, n.d., <http://www.yellowstone-natl-park.com/> (November 27, 2006).

2. John Muir, "Chapter II: The Yellowstone National Park," *Sierra Club,* n.d., <http://www.sierraclub.org/john_muir_exhibit/frameindex.html?http://www.sierraclub.org/John_Muir_Exhibit/writings/our_national_parks/chapter_2.html> (January 3, 2007).

3. Yellowstone National Park, "Weather," *National Park Service,* n.d., <www.nps.gov/yell/planyourvisit/weather.htm> (January 3, 2007).

4. "New Books," *University of California Botanical Garden,* vol. 25, no. 4, Fall 2000, p. 7, <http://72.14.209.104/search?q=cache:VWwPvKR4oG4J:botanicalgarden.berkeley.edu/newsletter_pdfs/fallnews2000.pdf+%22bitter+and+nauseous+to+the+palate&hl=en&gl=us&ct=clnk&cd=1&ie=UTF-8> (January 3, 2007).

## Chapter 5. Hot-Button Issues

1. Amanda Griscom, "Snowmobiling through Yellowstone," salon.com, February 19, 2004, <http://dir.salon.com/story/opinion/feature/2004/02/19/yellowstone/index.html> (December 1, 2006).

2. Rachel Odell, "Farm Bureau mulls appeal in landmark wolf ruling," yellowstoneparknet.com, January 20, 2000, <http://www.yellowstoneparknet.com/articles/wolves_2.php> (December 2, 2006).

3. Tim Springer, interview by author, e-mail, October 26, 2006.

4. Don Knapp, "Yellowstone bison roam into killing fields," *CNN Interactive,* February 17, 1997, <http://www.cnn.com/EARTH/9702/18/buffalo.wars/index.html> (January 3, 2007).

5. Jim Robbins, "Anger Over Culling of Yellowstone's Bison," *The New York Times,* March 23, 2008, <http://www.nytimes.com/2008/03/23/us/23bison.html> (March 24, 2008).

6. Griscom, (accessed December 5, 2006).

7. Ibid.

## Chapter 6. Endless Adventures

1. David Strege, "A fly-fisher's nirvana," *The Orange County Register,* August 15, 2006, <http://www.ocregister.com/ocregister/sports/homepage/article_1243039.php> (January 3, 2007).

2. "Trip Notes: Things to Do on a Yellowstone Vacation," YellowstonePark.com, March 13, 2006, <http://www.yellowstonepark.com/blog/TripNotes/> (December 9, 2006).

3. "Top 10 Things to see in YNP," Yellowstone National Park, n.d., <http://www.yellowstone.net/topten.htm> (March 14, 2008).

4. Mike Stark, "New park lights don't upstage night sky," *Billings Gazette,* May 9, 2003, <http://www.billingsgazette.com/newdex.php?displayrednews/2003/05/09/build/wyoming/30 lights.inc> (December 10, 2006).

5. Yellowstone National Park, "Hiking in the park," National Park Service, n.d., <http://www.nps.gov/yell/planyourvisit/hiking.htm> (January 3, 2007).

6. Strege.

7. Ibid.

8. "Trip Notes: Things to Do on a Yellowstone Vacation."

Apel, Melanie Ann. *The Yellowstone Park Fire of 1988.* New York: Rosen Publishing Group, Inc., 2004.

Becker, John E. *The North American Bison.* San Diego, Calif.: Kidhaven Press, 2003.

Bryan, T. Scott. *Geysers: What They Are and How They Work.* Missoula, Mont.: Mountain Press Publishing Company, 2005.

Franke, Mary Ann. *To Save the Wild Bison: Life on the Edge in Yellowstone.* Norman, Okla.: University of Oklahoma Press, 2005.

Hamilton, John. *Yellowstone National Park.* Edina, Minn.: ABDO Publishing, 2005.

Hines, Gary. *Midnight Forests: A Story of Gifford Pinchot and our National Forests.* Honesdale, Pa.: Boyds Mill Press, 2005.

Patent, Dorothy Hinshaw. Photographs by Dan and Cassie Hartman. *When the Wolves Returned: Restoring Nature's Balance in Yellowstone.* New York: Walker, 2008.

Petersen, Christine. *Land Preservation.* New York: Children's Press, 2004.

Smith, Douglas W. & Gary Ferguson. *Decade of the Wolf: Returning the Wild to Yellowstone.* Guilford, Conn.: Lyons Press, 2005.

**A**

activities available, 14, 91–93, 104–116
admission fees, 7
Albright Visitor Center and Museum, 113
amphibians, 79
animal species, 14, 66–73. *See also specific animals.*
antelope (pronghorns), 57, 68, 73, 102
Artist Point, 98
attendance, 7, 11–12, 45–48
automobiles, 44–45, 47

**B**

bald eagles, 14, 77–78, 102
Bear Management Guidelines, 104
bears
    black, 49, 67–68
    grizzly, 49, 67–68, 81, 99, 102
    safety, 104–106
bighorn sheep, 21, 73
biking, 108
Biosphere Reserve Site designation, 6, 50
birds, 77–78, 102
Biscuit Basin Loop, 115
bison, 41, 61, 70–71, 86–89, 102
bitterroot, 66
black bears, 49, 67–68
Blackfeet Indians, 22
boating, 107–108
boreal toad, 79
Bridger, Jim, 25–27
brucellosis, 86–89
Bush, George W., 93

**C**

cacti, 64
calderas, 7, 19
camping, 104–106
Canary Spring, 99
Cheney, Dick, 93
chorus frog, 79
Clagett, William, 34–35
Clark, William, 23
Clinton, Bill, 92
Colter, John, 23
Columbia spotted frog, 79
controversy overview, 81–82

Cook, Charles W., 27–30
coyotes, 14, 42, 71–72, 83–84, 99, 102
Crow Indians, 22
Crystal Falls waterfall, 98
cutthroat trout, 76, 91

**E**

Eagle Peak, 6
Earthquake Lake, 48
earthquakes, 6, 47–48
Echinus geyser, 101
ecological issues
    bison management, 86–89
    invasive species, 89–91
    overgrazing, 84–85
    snowmobilers, 91–93
    tourism, 48–50, 79
    wolf restoration, 83–84
elk, 11, 14, 37–38, 52, 61, 68–70, 84–86, 99, 102
Emerald hot spring, 101
employees, 7
entrance fees/permits, 96
Everts, Truman, 31
exploration, 23–33

**F**

fact sheet, 6–7
fairy slipper, 66
Firehole Hotel, 43
Firehole River, 109
fires of 1988, 51–53
fishing, 14, 49, 73–76, 101, 102, 108–109
Fishing Bridge, 49, 73
flowers, 64, 66
Folsom, David, 27–30
food, 112–113
foothills, 60–61
Fountain Hotel, 43
Fountain Paint Pots, 103
fringed gentian, 66
frogs, 79
fumaroles, 20, 60, 102–103

**G**

gas/oil, 49
geysers, 6, 9–10, 30, 59–60, 97–98. *See also specific geysers.*
Giantess, 30
glacier lilies, 64

Grand Canyon of Yellowstone, 58–59, 98, 111
Grand Teton National Park, 46, 77, 96, 116–117
gray wolves, 71, 82–86, 102, 114
Greater Yellowstone Ecosystem, 11, 52, 64
Green Dragon hot spring, 101
grizzly bears, 49, 67–68, 81, 99, 102
Gunnison, J. W., 26

**H**
Hayden Valley, 58, 99
hiking, 14, 102, 106–107
history
    Army control, 41–42
    automobiles, 44–45, 47
    earthquake, 47–48
    fires of 1988, 51–53
    hunting, 37–40
    infrastructure improvement, 39
    railroads, 40–41
    rangers, 44
    vandalization, 38–40
horseback riding, 14, 109–110
hotels, 43, 111–112
hot springs. *See also* Mammoth Hot Springs.
    described, 24, 55, 60
    evolution of, 20, 101
    as survival tool, 31
    vandalism of, 40
humans (first), arrival of, 20–22
hunting, 37–40
hydrothermal features, 6, 60, 101–103, 106, 113, 115–116

**I**
Indian paintbrush, 65

**L**
Lacey Act, 41
lake trout, 76, 91
Lake Yellowstone Hotel, 112
Lamar Valley, 57–58, 102, 110, 114
Langford, Nathaniel P., 31, 37
Lewis, Meriwether, 23
Liberty Cap, 99
lightning storms, 63–64
lizards, 79
lodgepole pines, 61, 64

lodging, 43, 111–112
logging, 49
Louisiana Purchase, 23
Lower Falls/Yellowstone River, 7, 98
Lower Geyser Basin, 102–103

**M**
Madison River, 109
mailing address, 7
Mallard Creek Loop, 115
Mammoth Hot Springs, 56, 99, 110, 114
map, 5
Mission 66, 47
moose, 60, 72, 102
Moran, Thomas, 33, 102
Morning Glory Pool, 96
mud pots, 20, 60, 102–103
Muir, John, 14, 55, 58
mule deer, 72–73
museums/visitor centers, 113

**N**
National Hotel, 43
National Park Bill, 34–35
National Park Service (NPS), 44
natural fire policy, 51–52
New Zealand mud snail, 89–90
Norris, Philetus, 39
Norris Geyser Basin, 101

**O**
Old Faithful geyser, 10–11, 30–31, 97–98
Old Faithful Inn, 43, 112
Old Faithful Visitor Center, 113
Old West Dinner Cookout, 113
ospreys, 78, 102
overgrazing, 84–85

**P**
Palette Spring, 99
parasites, 90–91
park facilities, 7, 113
Pelican Valley, 58
Peterson, William, 27–30
picnicking, 110–111
plant life (flora), 64–66. *See also* *specific plants.*
prairie rattlesnake, 79
pronghorns (antelope), 57, 68, 73, 102

**R**

railroads, 40–41
rangers, 44
Raynolds, W. F., 26–27
Reese Creek, 6
reptiles, 79
rhyolite, 18, 58
riparian zones, 60
Roosevelt, Theodore, 57
Russell, Osborne, 25

**S**

safety issues, 104–107, 115–116
sagebrush lizard, 79
Sheep Eaters (Tukuaduka), 20–21
Shoshone Indians, 20–21
sightseeing, 14, 96, 114–115
skiing, 14, 114–116
snakes, 79
snowmobilers, 91–93, 115
South Rim Trail, 98
stay length, recommended, 96–97
Steamboat geyser, 101
swimming, 100

**T**

tiger salamander, 79
tourism
    activities available, 14, 91–93,
        104–116
    automobiles, 44–45, 47
    ecological issues (*See* ecological
        issues)
    nineteenth-century, 42–43
    twentieth-century, 45–48
    wolf watching, 84, 114
tours, 96, 114–115
Tower Fall/Creek, 102
trees, 60–61, 64
trout, 76, 91, 101
Trudeau, Jean Baptiste, 23
trumpeter swans, 78

**U**

undulant fever, 86
UNESCO, 50
Upper Falls waterfall, 98
Upper Geyser Basin, 97–98

**V**

vandalization, 38–40
visitor centers/museums, 113

**W**

wandering garter snake, 79
Washburn, Henry D., 30
waterfalls, 7, 98, 99, 102
water sports, 107–108
weather, 6, 61–64, 104, 115–116
West Thumb Geyser Basin, 103
whirling disease, 90–91
White Dome geyser, 103
wildlife (fauna), 14, 66–73. *See
    also specific animals.*
winter sports, 114–116
Wolf Restoration Management
    plan, 83
wolf watching, 84, 114
wolves, 71, 82–86, 102, 114
World Heritage Site designation,
    6, 50

**Y**

yellow monkey flower, 66
Yellowstone Lake, 7, 14, 58, 91,
    99–101, 110
Yellowstone National Park
    as America's Getaway, 12–14
    Biosphere Preserve/World
        Heritage Site designations,
        6, 50
    creation/evolution of, 17–20
    designation as, 6, 11, 33–35
    entrances/roads/trails, 7
    geographic features, 6–7, 11
    towns nearest to, 117
    traveling to, 95–96
Yellowstone River, 58, 99, 109